A Discourse on Meekness and Quietness of Spirit

Matthew Henry

(1662-1714)

"A meek and quiet spirit, which is in the
sight of God of great price." 1 Peter 3:4

THE NATURE OF MEEKNESS AND QUIETNESS OF SPIRIT

Meekness and quietness seem to imply much the same thing, but as the latter has something of metaphor in it, it will illustrate the former, so we shall speak of them distinctly.

We must be of a MEEK spirit. Meekness is easiness of spirit: not a sinful easiness to be debauched, as Ephraim's, who willingly walked after the commandment of the idolatrous princes; nor a simple easiness to be imposed upon and deceived, as Rehoboam's, who, when he was forty years old, is said to be young and tender-hearted; but a gracious easiness to be wrought upon by that which is good, as theirs whose heart of stone is taken away and to whom a heart of flesh is given. Meekness accommodates the soul to every occurrence, and so makes a man easy to himself and to all about him. The Latins call a meek man mansuetus, which refers to the taming and reclaiming of creatures wild by nature, and bringing them to be tractable and familiar. James 3:7, 8. Man's corrupt nature has made him like the wild donkey used to the wilderness, or the swift dromedary traversing her ways. Jer. 2:23, 24. But when the grace of meekness gets dominion in the soul, it alters the temper of it, submits it to management; and now the wolf dwells with the lamb, and the leopard lies down with the kid, and a little child may lead them; for enmities are laid aside, and there is nothing to hurt or destroy. Isa. 11:6, 9.

Meekness may be considered with respect both to God and to our brethren; it belongs to both the tables of the law, and attends upon the first great commandment, You shall love the Lord your God; as well as the second, which is like it, You shall love your neighbor as yourself; though its special reference is to the latter.

I. There is MEEKNESS TOWARDS God, and it is the easy and quiet submission of the soul to His whole will, according as He is pleased to make it known, whether by His word or by His providence.

1. It is the silent submission of the soul to the word of God: the understanding bowed to every divine truth, and the will to every divine precept; and both without murmuring or arguing. The word is then an "engrafted word," when it is received with meekness, that is, with a sincere willingness to be taught, and desire to learn. Meekness is a grace that cuts the stock, and holds it open, that the word, as a shoot, may be grafted in; it breaks up the fallow ground, and makes it fit to receive the seed; captivates the high thoughts, and lays the soul like white paper under God's pen. When the dayspring takes hold of the ends of the earth, it is said to be turned as clay to the seal. Job 38:14. In the same way, meekness disposes the soul to admit the rays of divine light, which before it rebelled against; it opens the heart, as Lydia's was opened, and sets us down with Mary at the feet of Christ, the learner's place and posture.

The promise of teaching is made to the meek, because they are disposed to learn: "the meek He will teach His way." The word of God is gospel indeed, "good tidings to the meek;" they will entertain it and welcome it. The "poor in spirit" are evangelized; and Wisdom's alms are given to those that with meekness wait daily at her gates, and like beggars wait at the doorposts. Prov. 8:34. The language of this meekness is that of the child Samuel: "Speak, Lord, for

Your servant hears;" and that of Joshua, who, when he was in that high post of honor, giving command to Israel, and bidding defiance to all their enemies—his breast filled with great and bold thoughts—yet, upon the hint of a message from heaven, thus submits himself to it: "What does my Lord say to His servant?" and that of Paul—and it was the first breath of the new man—"Lord, what will You have me to do?" and that of Cornelius: "And now we are all here present before God, to hear all that you have been commanded by the Lord;" and that of the good man I have read of, who, when he was going to hear the word, used to say, "Now let the word of the Lord come; and if I had six hundred necks, I would bow them all to the authority of it." To receive the word with meekness, is to be delivered into it as into a mold: this seems to be Paul's metaphor in Rom. 6:17, that "form of doctrine which was delivered you." Meekness softens the wax, that it may receive the impression of the seal, whether it be for doctrine or reproof, for correction or instruction in righteousness. It opens the ear to discipline, silences objections, and suppresses the risings of the carnal mind against the word; agreeing with the law that it is good and esteeming all the precepts concerning all things to be right, even when they give the greatest check to flesh and blood.

True meekness will prevent us from opposing either the obvious parts of Scripture, severely as they may denounce our vices, or the mysterious parts, in reading which vanity may suggest that we could have dictated what is more profitable. Augustine.

2. It is the silent submission of the soul to the providence of God, for that also is the will of God concerning us.

1. When the events of Providence are grievous and afflicting, displeasing to sense and opposing our worldly interests, meekness not only quiets us under them, but reconciles us to them; and enables us not only to bear, but to receive evil as well as good at the hand of the Lord; which is the excellent frame that Job argues himself into: it is to kiss the rod, and even to accept the punishment of our sin, taking all in good part that God does; not daring to contend with our Maker, no, nor desiring to advise Him, but being dumb, and not opening the mouth, because God does it. How meek was Aaron under the severe dispensation which took away his sons with a particular mark of divine wrath. He "held his peace." God was sanctified, and therefore Aaron was satisfied, and had not a word to say against it. How unlike this was the temper, or rather the distemper of David, who was not like a man after God's own heart when he was displeased because the Lord had made a breach upon Uzzah—as if God must have asked David permission to assert the honor of his ark. When God's anger is kindled, our anger must be stifled; such is the law of meekness, that whatever pleases God must not displease us. David was in a better frame when he penned the 56th Psalm, the title of which, some think, speaks of his calm and submissive spirit when the Philistines took him in Gath. It is entitled, The Silent Dove Afar Off. It was his calamity that he was afar off, but he was then as a silent dove—mourning perhaps, Isa.38:14—but not murmuring, not struggling, not resisting, when seized by the birds of prey; and the psalm he penned in this frame was Michtam, a golden psalm. The language of this meekness is that of Eli, "It is the Lord;" and that of David to the same purport, "Here am I; let Him do to me as seems good to Him." Not only, He can do what He will, subscribing to His power, for who can stay His hand? or, He may do what He will, subscribing to His sovereignty,

for He gives not account of any of His matters; or, He will do what He will, subscribing to His unchangeableness, for He is of one mind, and who can turn Him? but, Let him do what He will, subscribing to His wisdom and goodness, as Hezekiah, "Good is the word of the Lord, which you have spoken." Let Him do what He will, for He will do what is best; and therefore if God should refer the matter to me, says the meek and quiet soul, being well assured that He knows what is good for me better than I do for myself, I would refer it to Him again: "He shall choose our inheritance for us."

2. When the methods of Providence are dark and intricate, and we are quite at a loss what God is about to do with us—His way is in the sea, and His path in the great waters, and His footsteps are not known, clouds and darkness are round about Him—a meek and quiet spirit acquiesces in an assurance that all things shall work together for good to us, if we love God, though we cannot understand how or which way. It teaches us to follow God with an implicit faith, as Abraham did when he went out, not knowing where he went, but knowing very well whom he followed. It quiets us with this, that though what He does we know not now, yet we shall know hereafter. John 13:7. When poor Job was brought to that dismal plunge, that he could no way trace the footsteps of divine Providence, but was almost lost in the labyrinth, Job 23:8, 9, how quietly does he sit down with this thought: "But He knows the way that I take: when He has tried me, I shall come forth as gold."

II. There is MEEKNESS TOWARDS OUR BRETHREN, towards "all men." Tit. 3:2. Meekness is especially conversant about the disposition of anger: not to entirely destroy and erase from the soul the holy indignation of which the Scriptures speak, for that were to quench a coal which sometimes there is occasion for, even at God's altar, and to blunt the edge even of the spiritual weapons with which we are to carry on our spiritual warfare; but its office is to direct and govern this affection, that we may be angry and not sin. Eph. 4:26.

Meekness, in the school of the philosophers, is a virtue consisting in a mean between the extremes of rash excessive anger on the one hand, and a defect of anger on the other; a mean which Aristotle confesses it very hard exactly to gain.

Meekness, in the school of Christ, is one of the fruits of the Spirit. Gal. 5:22, 23. It is a grace wrought by the Holy Spirit both as a sanctifier and as a comforter in the hearts of all true believers, teaching and enabling them at all times to keep their passions under the conduct and government of religion and right reason. I observe that it is worked in the hearts of all true believers, because, though there are some whose natural temper is unhappily sour and harsh, yet wherever there is true grace, there is a disposition to strive against, and strength in some measure to conquer such a disposition. And though in this, as in other graces, an absolute sinless perfection cannot be expected in this present state, yet we are to labor after it, and press towards it.

More particularly, the work and office of meekness is to enable us to prudently govern our own anger when at any time we are provoked, and to patiently bear the anger of others, that it may not provoke us. The former is its office especially in superiors, the latter in inferiors, and both in equals.

1. Meekness teaches us prudently to govern our own anger whenever anything occurs that is provoking. As it is the work of temperance to moderate our natural appetites in things that are pleasing to sense, so it is the work of meekness to moderate our natural passions against those things that are displeasing to sense, and to guide and govern our resentments. Anger in the soul is like mettle in a horse, good if it is well managed. Now meekness is the bridle, as wisdom is the hand that gives law to it, puts it into the right way, and keeps it in an even, steady, and regular pace; reducing it when it turns aside, preserving it in a due decorum, and restraining it and giving it restraint when at any time it grows headstrong and outrageous, and threatens mischief to ourselves or others. It must thus be held in, like the horse and mule, with bit and bridle, lest it break the hedge, run over those that stand in its way, or throw the rider himself headlong. It is true of anger, as we say of fire, that it is a good servant but a "bad master;" it is good on the hearth, but bad in the hangings. Meekness keeps it in its place, sets banks to this sea, and says, This far you shall come, and no further; here shall your proud waves stop.

In reference to our own anger, when at any time we meet with the excitements of it, the work of meekness is to do these four things:

1. To consider the circumstances of that which we perceive to be a provocation, so as at no time to express our displeasure except upon due mature deliberation. The office of meekness is to keep reason upon the throne in the soul as it ought to be; to preserve the understanding clear and unclouded, the judgment untainted and unbiased in the midst of the greatest provocations, so as to be able to set every thing in its true light, and to see it in its own color,

and to determine accordingly; as also to keep silence in the court, that the "still small voice" in which the Lord is, as He was with Elijah at mount Horeb, may not be drowned by the noise of the tumult of the passions.

A meek man will never be angry at a child, at a servant, at a friend, until he has first seriously weighed the cause in just and even balances, while a steady and impartial hand holds the scales, and a free and unprejudiced thought judges it necessary. It is said of our Lord Jesus, John 11:33, He troubled Himself; which denotes it to be a considerate act, and what He saw reason for. Things go right in the soul, when no resentments are admitted into the affections but what have first undergone the scrutiny of the understanding, and thence received their pass. That passion which does not come in by this door, but climbs up some other way, the same is a thief and a robber, against which we should guard. In a time of war—and such a time it is in every sanctified soul, in a constant war between grace and corruption—due care must be taken to examine all travelers, especially those that come armed: where they came from, where they go, whom they are for, and what they would have. Thus should it be in the well-governed, well-disciplined soul. Let meekness stand sentinel; and upon the advance of a provocation, let us examine who it is that we are about to be angry with, and for what. What are the merits of the cause; where does the offense lie; what was the nature and tendency of it? What are likely to be the consequences of our resentments; and what harm will it be if we stifle them, and let them go no further? Such as these are the questions which meekness would put to the soul; and in answer to them it would remove all which passion is apt to suggest, and hear reason only as it becomes rational creatures to do.

Three great dictates of meekness we find put together in one scripture: "Be swift to hear, slow to speak, slow to wrath;" which some observe to be couched in three proper names of Ishmael's sons, Gen. 25:14; 1 Chr. 1:30—which Bishop Prideaux, in the beginning of the wars, recommended to a gentleman that had been his pupil, as the summary of his advice—Mishma, Dumah, Massa; the signification of which is, hear, keep silence, bear. Hear reason, keep passion silent, and then you will not find it difficult to bear the provocation.

It is said of the Holy One of Israel, when the Egyptians provoked Him, He weighed a path to His anger; so the margin reads it from the Hebrew, Psa. 78:50. Justice first poised the cause, and then anger poured out the vials. Thus the Lord came down to see the pride of the Babel-builders before He scattered them, and to see the wickedness of Sodom before He overthrew it—though both were obvious and barefaced—to teach us to consider before we are angry, and to judge before we pass sentence, that herein we may be followers of God as dear children, and be merciful, as our Father which is in heaven is merciful.

We read of the "meekness of wisdom;" for where there is not wisdom—that wisdom which is profitable to direct, that wisdom of the prudent which is to understand his way—meekness will not long be preserved. It is our rashness and inconsideration that betray us to all the mischiefs of an ungoverned passion, on the neck of which the reins are laid which should be kept in the hand of reason, and so we are hurried upon a thousand precipices. Nehemiah is a remarkable instance of prudence presiding in just resentments: he owns, "I was very angry when I heard their cry;" but that anger did not at all transgress the laws of meekness, for it follows, "then I consulted with myself," or as the Hebrew has it, my heart consulted in me. Before he expressed his displeasure he retired into his own bosom, took time for sober thought upon the case, and then he rebuked the nobles in a very solid, rational discourse, and the success was good. In every cause when passion demands immediate judgment, meekness moves for further time, and will have the matter fairly argued, and counsel heard on both sides.

When Job had any quarrel with his servants, he was willing to admit a rational debate of the matter, and to hear what they had to say for themselves; for he says, "What shall I do when God rises up?" And withal, "Did not He that made me in the womb, make him?" When our hearts are at any time hot within us, we should do well to put that question to ourselves which God put to Cain, Gen. 4:6. Why am I angry? Why am I angry at all? Why so soon angry? Why so very angry? Why so far transported and dispossessed of myself by my anger? What reason is there for all this? Do I well to be angry for a gourd, that came up in a night and perished in a night? Jonah 4:9. Should I be touched to the quick by such a sudden and transient provocation? Will not my cooler thoughts correct these hasty resentments, and therefore were it not better to check them now? Such are the reasonings of the meekness of wisdom.

2. The work of meekness is to calm the spirit, so as that the inward peace may not be disturbed by any outward provocation. No doubt a man may express his displeasure against the miscarriages of another, as much as at any time there is occasion for, without suffering his resentments to recoil upon himself, and throw his own soul into a fury. What need is there for a man to tear himself—his soul, as it is in the Hebrew—in his anger? Job 18:4. Cannot we

charge home upon our enemy camp without the willful disordering of our own troops? Surely we may, if meekness has the command; for that is a grace which keeps a man master of himself while he contends to be master of another, and fortifies the heart against the assaults of provocation that do us no great harm while they do not rob us of our peace, nor disturb the rest of our souls. As patience in case of sorrow, so meekness in case of anger keeps possession of the soul, as the expression is in Luke 21:19, that we be not dispossessed of that freehold. The drift of Christ's farewell sermon to his disciples we have in the first words of it, "Let not your hearts be troubled." John 14:1. It is the duty and interest of all good people, whatever happens, to keep trouble from their hearts, and to have them even and sedate, though the eye, as Job expresses it, should "continue" unavoidably "in the provocation" of this world. "The wicked"—the turbulent and unquiet, as the world primarily signifies—"are like the troubled sea when it cannot rest;" but that peace of God which passes all understanding, keeps the hearts and minds of all the meek of the earth. Meekness preserves the mind from being ruffled and discomposed, and the spirit from being unhinged by the vanities and vexations of this lower world. It stills the noise of the sea, the noise of her waves, and the tumult of the soul; it permits not the passions to crowd out in a disorderly manner, like a confused, ungoverned rabble, but draws them out like the trained bands, every one in his own order, as wisdom and grace give the word of command.

3. Meekness will curb the tongue, and "keep the mouth as with a bridle" when the heart is hot. Even when there may be occasion for a keenness of expression, and we are called to rebuke sharply—cuttingly, Titus 1:13—yet meekness forbids all fury and indecency of language, and

every thing that sounds like clamor and evil-speaking. The meekness of Moses was not at hand when he spoke that unadvised word "rebels," for which he was shut out of Canaan, though rebels they were, and at that time very provoking. Men in a passion are apt to give reviling language, to call names, and those most senseless and ridiculous—to take the blessed name of God in vain, and so profane it. It is a wretched way by which the children of hell vent their passion at their beasts, their servants, any person, or any thing that provokes them, to swear at them. Men in a passion are apt to reveal secrets, to make rash vows and resolutions, which afterwards prove a snare, and sometimes to slander and belie their brethren, and bring railing accusations, and so do the devil's work; and to speak that "in their haste" concerning others, Psalm 116:11, of which they afterwards see cause to repent. How brutishly did Saul in his passion call his own son, the heir-apparent to the crown, the "son of the perverse rebellious woman." "Racca" and "you fool" are specified by our Savior as breaches of the law of the sixth commandment; and the passion in the heart is so far from excusing such opprobrious speeches—for which purpose it is commonly alleged—that really it is that which gives them their malignity: they are the smoke from that fire, the gall and wormwood springing from that root of bitterness; and if for "every idle word that men speak," much more for such wicked words as these, must they give an account at the day of judgment. And as it is a reflection upon God to kill, so it is to curse men that are made after the image of God, though ever so much our inferiors; that is, to speak ill of them, or to wish ill to them.

This is the disease which meekness prevents, and is in the tongue a "law of kindness." It is to the tongue as the helm is to the ship, Jas. 3:4, not to silence it, but to guide it, to steer it wisely, especially when the wind is high. If at any time we have conceived passion and thought evil, meekness will lay the hand upon the mouth—as the wise man's advice is, Prov. 30:32—to keep that evil thought from venting itself in any evil word reflecting upon God or our brother. It will reason a disputed point without noise, give a reproof without a reproach, convince a man of his folly without calling him a fool, will teach superiors either to forbear threatening, Eph. 6:9, or, as the margin reads it, to moderate it; and will look diligently lest any root of bitterness, springing up, trouble us, and thereby we and many others become defiled.

4. Meekness will cool the heat of passion quickly, and not allow it to continue. As it keeps us from being soon angry, so it teaches us when we are angry to be soon pacified. The anger of a meek man is like fire struck out of steel—hard to get out; and when it is, soon gone. The wisdom that is from above, as it is "gentle," and so not apt to provoke, so it is "easy to be entreated" when any provocation is given, and has the ear always open to the first proposals and overtures of satisfaction, submission, and reconciliation; and thus the anger is turned away. He that is of a meek spirit will be quick to forgive injuries and affronts, and has some excuse or other ready with which to extenuate and qualify the provocation, which an angry man, for the exasperating and justifying of his own resentments, will industriously aggravate. It is but to say, "There is no great harm done; or if there is, there was none intended; and peradventure it was an oversight;" and so the offense, being looked at through that end of the perspective which diminishes, is easily passed by, and the distemper being taken in time, goes off quickly, the fire is quenched before it gets head, and by a speedy intervention the plague is stopped. While the world is so full of the sparks of

provocation, and there is so much tinder in the hearts of the best, no marvel if anger come sometimes into the bosom of a wise man; but it rests only in the bosom of fools. Eccl. 7:9. Angry thoughts as other vain thoughts may crowd into the heart upon a sudden surprise, but meekness will not suffer them to lodge there, nor let the sun go down upon the wrath, Eph. 4:26; for if it does, there is danger lest it rise bloody the next morning. Anger concocted becomes malice; it is the wisdom of meekness, by proper applications, to disperse the humor before it comes to a head. One would have thought, when David so deeply resented Nabal's abuse, that nothing less than the blood of Nabal and all his house could have quenched his rage; but it was done at a cheaper rate; and he showed his meekness by yielding to the diversion that Abigail's present and speech gave him, and that with satisfaction and thankfulness. He was not only soon pacified, but blessed her, and blessed God for her that pacified him. God does not contend forever, neither is He always angry; "His anger endures but a moment." How unlike Him are those whose sword devours forever, and whose anger burns like the coals of juniper! But the grace of meekness, if it fail of keeping the peace of the soul from being broken, yet fails not to recover it presently, and make up the breach; and upon the least transport, brings help in time of need, restores the soul, puts it in frame again, and no great harm is done. Such as these are the achievements of meekness in governing our own anger.

2. Meekness teaches and enables us patiently to bear the anger of others, which property of meekness we have especially occasion for in reference to our superiors and equals. Commonly that which provokes anger is anger, as fire kindles fire; now meekness prevents that violent collision which forces out these sparks, and softens at least

one side, and so puts a stop to a great deal of mischief; for it is the second blow that makes the quarrel. Our first concern should be to prevent the anger of others by giving no offense to any, but becoming all things to all men, everyone studying to please his neighbor for good to edification, Rom. 15:2, and endeavoring as much as lies in us to accommodate ourselves to the temper of all with whom we have to do, and to make ourselves acceptable and agreeable to them. How easy and comfortable should we make every relation and all our dealings if we were but better acquainted with this are of obliging. Naphtali's tribe, that was famous for giving goodly words, Gen. 49:21, had the happiness of being satisfied with favor, Deut. 33:23; for "every man shall kiss his lips that gives a right answer." In the conjugal relation it is taken for granted that the care of the husband is to please his wife, and the care of the wife is to please her husband, 1 Cor. 7:33, 34; and where there is that mutual care, enjoyment cannot be lacking. Some people love to be unkind, and take a pleasure in displeasing, and especially contrive to provoke those they find passionate and easily provoked, that—as he that gives his neighbor drink, and puts his bottle to him, Hab. 2:15, 16—they may look upon his shame, to which, in his passion, he exposes himself; and so they make a mock at sin, and become like the madman that casts firebrands, arrows, and death, and says, "Am not I in sport?" But the law of Christ forbids us to provoke one another, unless it is "to love and good works;" and enjoins us to "bear one another's burdens, and so fulfill the law of Christ."

But because they must rise early who will please everybody, and carry their cup even indeed who will give no offense, our next concern must be to behave ourselves in such a way that when others are angry, that we may not make bad worse. And this is one principal thing in which the younger must submit themselves to the elder; no, in which all of us must be "subject one to another," as our rule is in 1 Pet. 5:5. And here meekness is of use, either to enjoin silence or indite a soft answer.

1. To enjoin silence. It is prescribed to servants to please their masters well in all things, "not answering again," for that is displeasing: better say nothing than say that which is provoking. When our hearts are hot within us, it is good for us to keep silence, and hold our peace: so David did; and when he did speak, it was in prayer to God, and not in reply to the wicked that were before him. If the heart is angry, angry words will inflame it the more, as wheels are heated by a rapid motion. One reflection and repartee begets another, and the beginning of the debate is like the letting forth of water, which is with difficulty stopped when the least breach is made in the bank; and therefore meekness says, "By all means keep silence, and leave it off before it is meddled with." When a fire is begun, it is good, if possible, to smother it, and so prevent its spreading. Let us deal wisely, and stifle it in the birth, lest afterwards it prove too strong to be dealt with. Anger in the heart is like the books stowed in cellars in the conflagration of London, which, though they were extremely heated, never took fire until they took air many days after, which giving vent to the heat, put them into a flame. When the spirits are in a ferment, though it may be some present pain to check and suppress them, and the headstrong passions hardly admit the bridle, yet afterwards it will be no grief of heart to us.

Those who find themselves wronged and aggrieved, think they may have permission to speak; but it is better to be silent than to speak amiss, and make work for repentance. At such a time he that holds his tongue holds his peace; and if we soberly reflect, we shall find we have been often the worse for our speaking, but seldom the worse for our silence. This must be especially remembered and observed by as many as are under the yoke, who will certainly have most comfort in meekness and patience and silent submission, not only to the good and gentle, but also to the froward. It is good in such cases to remember our place, and if the spirit of a ruler rise up against us, not to leave it, that is, not to do any thing unbecoming; for yielding pacifies great offenses. Eccl. 10:4. We have a common proverb that teaches us this: "When you are the hammer, knock your fill; but when you are the anvil, lie still;" for it is the posture you are cut out for, and which best becomes you.

If others are angry with us without cause, and we have ever so much reason on our side, yet often it is best to delay our own vindication, though we think it necessary, until the passion is over; for there is nothing said or done in passion, but it may be better said and better done afterwards. When we are calm, we shall be likely to say it and do it in a better manner; and when our brother is calm, we shall be likely to say it and do it to a better purpose. A needful truth spoken in anger may do more hurt than good, and offend rather than satisfy. The prophet himself forbore even a message from God when he saw Amaziah in a passion. Sometimes it may be advisable to get some one else to say that for us which is to be said, rather than say it ourselves. However, we have a righteous God, to whom, if in a meek silence we allow ourselves to be injured, we may commit our cause, and having his promise that He will "bring forth our righteousness as the light, and our judgment as the noonday," we had better leave it in His hands than undertake to manage it ourselves, lest that which we call clearing ourselves, God should call quarreling with our brethren. David was greatly provoked by those that sought his hurt, and spoke mischievous things against him; and yet says he, "I, as a deaf man, heard not; I was as a dumb man, that opens not his mouth." And why so? It was not because he had nothing to say, or knew not how to say it, but because "in You, O Lord, do I hope: You will hear, O Lord my God." If God hear, what need have I to hear? His concerning Himself in the matter supersedes ours, and He is not only engaged in justice to own every righteous cause that is injured, but He is further engaged in honor to appear for those who, in obedience to the law of meekness, commit their cause to Him. If any vindication or avenging is necessary—which infinite Wisdom is the best judge of—He can do it better than we can; therefore "give place unto wrath," that is, to the judgment of God, which is according to truth and equity; make room for Him to take the seat, and do not step in before Him. It is fit that our wrath should stand by to give way to his, for the wrath of man engages not the righteousness of God for him. Even just appeals made to Him, if they are made in passion, are not admitted into the court of heaven, being not duly presented; that one thing, error, is sufficient to overrule them. Let not therefore those that do well and suffer for it, spoil their own vindication by mistiming and mismanaging it; but tread in the steps of the Lord Jesus, who, when He was reviled, reviled not again; when He suffered, He threatened not; but was as a lamb dumb before the shearers, and so committed Himself to Him that judges righteously. It is indeed a principal part of self-denial to be silent when we have enough to say, and provocation to say it; but if we do thus control our tongues out of a pure regard to peace and love, it will turn to a good account, and will be an evidence for us that we are Christ's disciples, having learned to deny ourselves. It is better by silence to yield to our brother who is, or has been, or may be our friend, than by angry speaking to yield to the devil, who has been, and is, and ever will be our sworn enemy.

2. To give a soft answer. This Solomon commends as a proper expedient to turn away wrath, while grievous words do but stir up anger. When any speak angrily to us, we must pause a while and study an answer, which, both for the matter and manner of it, may be mild and gentle. This brings water, while peevishness and provocation would but bring oil to the flame. Thus is death and life in the power of the tongue; it is either healing or killing, an antidote or a poison, according as it is used. When the waves of the sea beat on a rock, they batter and make a noise, but a soft sand receives them silently, and returns them without damage. A soft tongue is a wonderful specific, and has a very strange virtue in it. Solomon says, "It breaks the bone," that is, it qualifies those that were provoked, and makes them pliable; it "heaps coals of fire upon the head" of an enemy, not to burn him, but to melt him. "Hard words," we say, "break no bones;" but it seems soft ones do, and yet do no harm, as they calm an angry spirit and prevent its progress. A stone that falls on a wool-pack rests there, and rebounds not to do any further mischief; such is a meek answer to an angry question.

The good effects of a soft answer, and the bad consequences of a peevish one, are observable in the stories of Gideon and Jephthah: both of them, in the day of their triumphs over the enemies of Israel, were quarreled with by the Ephraimites, when the danger was past and the victory won, because they had not been called upon to engage in the battle. Gideon pacified them with a soft answer: "What have I done now in comparison to you?" magnifying their achievements and lessening his own, speaking honorably of them and meanly of himself: "Is not the gleaning of the grapes of Ephraim better than the vintage of Abiezer?" In which reply it is hard to say whether there was more of wit or wisdom; and the effect was very good: the Ephraimites were pleased, their anger turned away, a civil war prevented, and nobody could think the worse of Gideon for his mildness and self-denial. On the contrary, he won more true honor by his victory over his own passion, than he did by his victory over all the host of Midian; for he that has rule over his own spirit is better than the mighty. The angel of the Lord has pronounced him a "mighty man of valor;" and this his tame submission did not at all derogate from that part of his character. But Jephthah, who by many instances appears to be a man of a rough and hasty spirit, though enrolled among the eminent believers, Heb. 11:32—for all good people are not alike happy in their temper—when the Ephraimites in like manner quarrel with him, rallies them, rebukes them for their cowardice, boasts of his own courage, and challenges them to make good their cause. Judg. 12:2. They retort a scurrilous reflection upon Jephthah's country, as it is usual with passion to taunt and jeer: "You Gileadites are fugitives." From words they go to blows, and so great a matter does this little fire kindle, that there goes no less to quench the flame than the blood of forty-two thousand Ephraimites. All which had been happily prevented, if Jephthah had had but half as much meekness in his heart as he had reason on his side.

A soft answer is the dictate and dialect of that wisdom which is from above, which is peaceable, gentle, and easy to be entreated; and to recommend it to us, we have the pattern of good men, as that of Jacob's conduct to Esau. Though none is so hard to be won as a brother offended, yet, as he had prevailed with God by faith and prayer, so he prevailed with his brother by meekness and humility. We have also the pattern of angels, who, even when a rebuke was needful, dared not turn it into a railing accusation, dared not give any reviling language, not to the devil himself, but referred the matter to God: "The Lord rebuke you;" as that passage in Jude 9 is commonly understood. More so, we have the pattern of a good God, who, though He could plead against us with His great power, yet gives soft answers: witness His dealing with Cain when he was wroth and his countenance fallen, reasoning the case with him: "Why are you angry? If you do well, will you not be accepted?" With Jonah likewise when he was so discontented: "Is it right for you to be angry?" This is represented, in the parable of the prodigal son, by the conduct of the father towards the elder brother, who was so angry that he would not come in. The father did not say, "Let him stay out then;" but he came himself and entreated him, when he might have interposed his authority and commanded him, saying, "Son, you are ever with me." When a passionate contest is begun, there is a plague broke out: the meek man, like Aaron, takes his censer with the incense of a soft answer, steps in seasonably, and stays it.

This soft answer, in case we have committed a fault, though perhaps not culpable to the degree that we are charged with, must be penitent, humble, and submissive; and we must be ready to acknowledge our error, and not stand in it, or insist upon our own vindication; but rather aggravate than excuse it, rather condemn than justify ourselves. It will be a good evidence of our repentance towards God, to humble ourselves to our brethren whom we have offended, as it will be also a good evidence of our being forgiven of God, if we are ready to forgive those that have offended us; and such yielding pacifies great offenses. Meekness teaches us, as often as we trespass against our brother, to "turn again and say, I repent." An acknowledgment, in case of a willful affront, is perhaps as necessary to pardon, as, we commonly say, restitution is in case of wrong.

So much for the opening of the nature of meekness, which yet will receive further light from considering more particularly what is implied in—

QUIETNESS OF SPIRIT.

Quietness is the evenness, the composure and the rest of the soul, which speaks both the nature and the excellency of the grace of meekness. The greatest comfort and happiness of man is sometimes set forth by quietness. That peace of conscience which Christ has left for a legacy to his disciples, that present sabbatism of the soul which is an earnest of the rest that remains for the people of God, is called "quietness and assurance forever," and is promised as the effect of righteousness. So graciously has God been pleased to entwine interests with us, as to enjoin the same thing as a duty which He proposes and promises as a privilege. Justly may we say that we serve a good Master, whose "Yoke is easy:" it is not only easy, but sweet and gracious, so the word signifies; not only tolerable, but amiable and acceptable. Wisdom's ways are not only pleasant, but pleasantness itself, and all her paths are peace. It is the character of the Lord's people, both in respect to holiness and happiness, that, however they are branded as the troublers of Israel, they are "the quiet in the land." If every saint is made a spiritual prince, Rev. 1:6, having a dignity above others and a dominion over himself, surely he is like Seraiah, "a quiet prince." It is a reign with Christ, the transcendent Solomon, under the influence of whose golden scepter there is "abundance of peace as long as the moon endures," yes, and longer, for "of the increase of his government and peace there shall be no end." Quietness is recommended as a grace which we should be endued with, and a duty which we should practice. In the midst of all the affronts and injuries that are or can be offered us, we must keep our spirits sedate and undisturbed, and evidence by a calm and even and regular behavior that they are so. This is quietness. Our Savior has pronounced the blessing of adoption upon the peacemakers, Matt. 5:9; those that are for peace, as David professes himself to be, in opposition to those that delight in war. Psalm 120:7. Now, if charity is for peace-making, surely this "charity begins at home," and is for making peace there in the first place. Peace in our own souls is some conformity to the example of the God of peace, who, though He does not always give peace on this earth, yet evermore "makes peace in his own high places." This some think is the primary intention of that peace-making on which Christ commands the blessing: it is to have strong and hearty affections to peace, to be peaceably-minded. In a word, quietness of spirit is the soul's stillness and silence from intending provocation to any, or resenting provocation from any with whom we have to do.

The word has something in it of metaphor, which admirably illustrates the grace of meekness.

1. We must be quiet as the air is quiet from winds. Disorderly passions are like stormy winds in the soul, they toss and hurry it, and often strand or overset it; they move it "as the trees of the forest are moved with the wind;" it is the prophet's comparison, and is an apt emblem of a man in passion. Now meekness restrains these winds, says to them, Peace, be still, and so preserves a calm in the soul, and makes it conformable to Him who has the winds in his hands, and is herein to be praised that even the stormy winds fulfill his word. A brisk gale is often useful,

especially to the ship of desire, as the Hebrew phrase is in Job 9:26; so there should be in the soul such a warmth and vigor as will help to speed us to the desired harbor. It is not well to lie wind-bound in dullness and indifference; but tempests are perilous, yes, though the wind is in the right point. So are strong passions, even in good men; they both hinder the voyage and hazard the ship. Such a quickness as consists with quietness is what we should all labor after, and meekness will contribute very much towards it; it will silence the noise, control the force, moderate the impetus, and correct undue and disorderly transports. What manner of grace is this, that even the winds and the sea obey it! If we will but use the authority God has given us over our own hearts, we may keep the winds of passion under the command of religion and reason; and then the soul is quiet, the sun shines, all is pleasant, serene, and smiling, and the man sleeps sweetly and safely on the lee-side. We make our voyage among rocks and quicksands, but if the weather is calm, we can the better steer so as to avoid them, and by a due care and temper strike the mean between extremes; whereas he that allows these winds of passion to get head, and spreads a large sail before them, while he shuns one rock, splits upon another, and is in danger of being drowned in destruction and perdition by many foolish and hurtful lusts, especially those whence wars and fightings come.

2. We must be quiet as the sea is quiet from waves. The wicked, whose sin and punishment both lie in the unruliness of their own souls, and the violence and disorder of their own passions, which perhaps will not be the least of their eternal torments, are compared to "the troubled sea, when it cannot rest, whose waters cast up mire and dirt;" that is, they are uneasy to themselves and to all about them, "raging waves of the sea, foaming out their own shame;"

their hard speeches which they speak against God and dignities and things which they know not, their great swelling words and mockings, Jude 13, 18, these are the shame they foam out. Now meekness is a grace of the Spirit, that moves upon the face of the waters and quiets them, smooths the ruffled sea and stills the noise of it; it casts forth none of the mire and dirt of passion. The waves mount not up to heaven in proud and vainglorious boasting; they go not down to the depths to scrape up vile and scurrilous language: there is no reeling to and fro, as men overcome with drink or with their own passion; there is none of that transport which brings them to their wits' end; but "they are glad because they are quiet; so He brings them to their desired haven." This calmness and evenness of spirit makes our passage over the sea of this world safe and pleasant, quick and speedy towards the desired harbor, and is amiable and exemplary in the eyes of others.

3. We must be quiet as the land is quiet from war. It was the observable happiness of Asa's reign, that "in his days the land was quiet." In the preceding reigns there was no peace to him that went out, or to him that came in; but now the rumors and alarms of war were stilled, and the people delivered from the noise of archers at the place of drawing waters, as when the land had rest in Deborah's time. Such a quietness there should be in the soul, and such a quietness there will be where meekness sways the scepter. A soul inflamed with wrath and passion upon all occasions, is like a kingdom embroiled in war, in a civil war, subject to continual frights and losses and perils; deaths and terrors in their most horrid shapes walk triumphantly, sleep is disturbed, families broken, friends suspected, enemies feared, laws silenced, commerce ruined, business neglected, cities wasted: such heaps upon heaps does ungoverned anger lay, when it is let loose in the

soul. But meekness makes these wars to cease, breaks the bow, cuts the spear, sheathes the sword, and in the midst of a contentious world preserves the soul from being the seat of war, and makes peace in her borders. The rest of the soul is not disturbed, its comforts not plundered, its government not disordered; the laws of religion and reason rule, and not the sword; neither its communion with God nor with the saints interrupted; no breaking in of temptation, no going out of corruption, no complaining in the streets; no occasion given, no occasion taken, to complain. Happy is the soul that is in such a case. The words of such wise men are heard in quiet, more than the cry of him that rules among fools, and this "wisdom is better than weapons of war." This is the quietness we should every one of us labor after; and it is what we might attain to, if we would but more support and exercise the authority of our graces, and guide and control the power of our passions.

4. We must be quiet as the child is quiet after weaning. It is the Psalmist's comparison: "I have behaved," or rather, I have composed, "and quieted myself as a child that is weaned of his mother; my soul is even as a weaned child." A child, while it is in the weaning, perhaps is a little cross and froward and troublesome for a time; but when it is perfectly weaned, how quickly does it accommodate itself to its new way of feeding. Thus a quiet soul, if provoked by the denial or loss of some earthly comfort or delight, quiets itself, and does not fret at it, nor perplex itself with anxious cares how to live without it, but composes itself to make the best of that which is. And this holy indifference to the delights of sense is, like the weaning of a child, a good step taken towards the perfect man, "the measure of the stature of the fullness of Christ." A child newly weaned is free from all the uneasiness and disquietude of care and fear and anger and revenge: how

undisturbed are its sleeps, and even in its dreams it looks pleasant and smiling. How easy its days; how quiet its nights. If put into a little sulk now and then, how soon it is over, the provocation forgiven, the sense of it forgotten, and both buried in an innocent kiss. Thus, if ever we would enter into the kingdom of heaven, we must be converted from pride, envy, ambition, and strife for precedency, and must become like little children. So our Savior has told us, who, even after His resurrection, is called "the holy child Jesus." And even when we have put away other childish things, yet still "in malice" we must be children. And as for the quarrels of others, a meek and quiet Christian endeavors to be as unselfish and as little engaged as a weaned child in the mother's arms, that is not capable of such angry resentments.

This is that meekness and quietness of spirit which is recommended to us: such a command and composure of the soul that it does not become unhinged by any provocation whatever, but all its powers and faculties preserved in due temper for the just discharge of their respective offices. In a word, put off all wrath and anger and malice, those corrupted limbs of the old man; pluck up and cast away those roots of bitterness, and stand upon a constant guard against all the exorbitances of your own passion: then you will soon know, to your comfort, better than I can tell you, what it is to be of a meek and quiet spirit.

THE EXCELLENCY OF MEEKNESS

The very opening of this cause, one would think, were enough to carry it; and the explaining of the nature of meekness and quietness should suffice to recommend it to us. Such an amiable sweetness does there appear in it upon the very first view, that if we look upon its beauty, we cannot but be enamored with it. But because of the opposition of our corrupt hearts to this, as well as the other graces of the Holy Spirit, I shall endeavor more particularly to show the excellency of it, that we may be brought, if possible, to be in love with it, and to submit our souls to its charming power.

It is said, that a man of understanding is of an excellent spirit. Prov. 17:27. Tremellius translates it, he is of a cool spirit; put them together and they teach us that a cool spirit is an excellent spirit, and that he is a man of understanding who is governed by such a spirit. The Scriptures tell us—what need we more?—That it is in the sight of God of great price, and we may be sure that is precious indeed which is so in God's sight: that is good, very good, which He pronounces so; for His judgment is according to truth, and sooner or later He will bring all the world to be of His mind; for as He has decided it, so shall our doom be, and, He will be "justified when He speaks, and clear when He judges."

The excellency of a meek and quiet spirit will appear, if we consider the credit of it, and the comfort of it—the present profit there is by it, and the preparedness there is in it for future blessings.

I. Consider how CREDITABLE a meek and quiet spirit is. Credit or reputation all desire, though few consider aright what it is, or what is the right way of obtaining it; and particularly it is little believed what a great deal of true honor there is in the grace of meekness, and what a sure and ready way mild and quiet souls take to gain the approval of their Master, and of all their fellow-servants who love Him and are like Him.

1. There is in it the credit of a victory. What a great figure do the names of high and mighty conquerors make in the records of fame! How are their conduct, their valor and success cried up and celebrated! But if we will believe the word of truth, and pass a judgment upon things according to it, "he that is slow to anger, is better than the mighty; and he that rules his spirit, than he that takes a city." Behold, a greater than Alexander or Caesar is here; the former of whom, some think, lost more true honor by yielding to his own ungoverned anger, than he got by all his conquests. No triumphant chariot so easy, so safe, so truly glorious, as that in which the meek and quiet soul rides over all the provocations of an injurious world with a gracious unconcernedness, no train so splendid, so noble, as that train of comforts and graces which attend this chariot. The conquest of an unruly passion is more honorable than that of an unruly people, for it requires more true courage. It is easier to kill an enemy without, which may be done at a blow, than to chain up and govern an enemy within, which requires a constant, even steady hand, and a long and regular management. It was more to the honor of David to yield himself conquered by Abigail's persuasions, than to have made himself a conqueror over Nabal and all his house. A rational victory must be more honorable to a rational creature than a brutal one. This is a cheap, safe, and unbloody conquest, that does nobody any harm; no

lives, no treasures are sacrificed to it; the glory of these triumphs are not stained, as others generally are, with funerals. Every battle of the warrior, says the prophet, "is with confused noise, and garments rolled in blood;" but this victory shall be obtained by the Spirit of the Lord of hosts. Yes, in meek and quiet suffering we are "more than conquerors," through Christ that loved us: conquerors with little loss, we lose nothing but the gratifying of a base lust; conquerors with great gain, the spoils we divide are very rich—the favor of God, the comforts of the Spirit, the foretastes of everlasting pleasures; these are more glorious and excellent than the mountains of prey. We are more than conquerors; that is, triumphers: we live a life of victory; every day is a day of triumph to the meek and quiet soul.

Meekness is a victory over ourselves and the rebellious lusts in our own bosoms; it is the quieting of internal conflicts, the stilling of an insurrection at home, which is often harder than to resist a foreign invasion. It is an effectual victory over those that injure us, and make themselves enemies to us, and is often a means of winning their hearts. The law of meekness is, If your enemy is hungry, feed him; if he is thirsty, not only give him a drink—which is an act of charity—but drink to him, in token of friendship and true love and reconciliation; and in so doing you shall "heap coals of fire upon his head," not to consume him, but to melt and soften him, that he may be cast into a new mold; and thus, while the angry and revengeful man, that will bear down all before him with a high hand, is overcome of evil, the patient and forgiving overcome evil with good; and forasmuch as their "ways please the Lord, He makes even their enemies to be at peace with them." Not only that, meekness is a victory over Satan, the greatest enemy of all; and what conquest can be more honorable than this? It is written for caution to us all, and it reflects honor on those who through grace overcome, that "we wrestle not against flesh and blood, but against principalities and powers, and the rulers of the darkness of this world." The magnifying of the adversary, magnifies the victory over him: such as these are the meek man's vanquished enemies; the spoils of these are the trophies of his victory. It is the design of the devil, that great deceiver and destroyer of souls, that is baffled; it is his attempt that is defeated, his assault that is repulsed, by our meekness and quietness. Our Lord Jesus was more admired for controlling and commanding the unclean spirits, than for any other cures which He wrought. Unruly passions are unclean spirits, legions of which some souls are possessed with, and desperate, outrageous work they make; the soul becomes like that miserable creature that cried and cut himself, Mark 5:5; or that, who was so often cast into the fire, and into the waters. Mark 9:22. The meek and quiet soul is, through grace, a conqueror over these enemies; their fiery darts are quenched by the shield of faith; Satan is in some measure trodden under his feet; and the victory will be complete shortly, when "he that overcomes" shall sit down with Christ upon His throne, even as He overcame, and is set down with the Father upon His throne, where He still appears in the emblem of His meekness, "a Lamb as it had been slain." And upon Mount Zion, at the head of his heavenly hosts, He appears also as a Lamb. Rev. 14:1. Such is the honor meekness has in those higher regions.

2. There is in it the credit of beauty. The beauty of a thing consists in the symmetry, harmony, and agreement of all the parts: now what is meekness but the soul's agreement with itself? It is the joint concurrence of all the affections to the universal peace and quiet of the soul, every one regularly acting in its own place and order, and

so contributing to the common good. Next to the beauty of holiness, which is the soul's agreement with God, is the beauty of meekness, which is the soul's agreement with itself. "Behold how good and how pleasant a thing it is" for the powers of the soul thus to "dwell together in unity;" the reason knowing how to rule, and the affections at the same time knowing how to obey. Exorbitant passion is a discord in the soul; it is like a tumor in the face which spoils the beauty of it: meekness scatters the humor, binds down the swelling, and so prevents the deformity and preserves the beauty. This is one instance of the loveliness of grace, "through My loveliness," says God to Israel, "which I had put upon you." It puts a charming loveliness and amiableness upon the soul, which renders it acceptable to all who know what true worth and beauty is. He that in righteousness and peace and joy in the Holy Spirit, that is, in Christian meekness and quietness of spirit, "serves Christ, is acceptable to God and approved of men." And to whom else can we wish to recommend ourselves?

Solomon, a very competent judge of beauty, has determined that it is "a man's wisdom" that "makes his face to shine;" and doubtless the meekness of wisdom contributes as much as any one branch of it to this luster. We read in Scripture of three whose faces shone remarkably, and they were all eminent for meekness. The face of Moses shone, and he was the meekest of all the men on earth. The face of Stephen shone, and he it was who, in the midst of a shower of stones, so meekly submitted, and prayed for his persecutors. The face of our Lord Jesus shone in his transfiguration, and he was the great pattern of meekness. It is a sweet and pleasing air which this grace puts upon the countenance, while it keeps the soul in tune, and frees it from those jarring discords which are the certain effect of an ungoverned passion.

3. There is in it the credit of an ornament. The apostle speaks of it as "an adorning" much more excellent and valuable than gold, pearls, or the most costly array. It is an adorning to the soul, the principal, the immortal part of the man. That outward adorning does but dress and beautify the body, which at the best is but a sister to the worms, and will soon be a feast for them; but this is the ornament of the soul, by which we are allied to the invisible world: it is an adorning that recommends us to God, which is in his sight "of great price." Ornaments go by estimation: now we may be sure the judgment of God is right and unerring. Every thing is indeed as it is with God: those are righteous indeed, that are righteous before God; and that is an ornament indeed, which He calls and counts so. It is an ornament of God's own making. Is the soul thus adorned? It is he that has adorned it. By his Spirit He has garnished the heavens, and by the same Spirit has He garnished the meek and quiet soul. It is an ornament of His accepting; it must be so, if it is of His own working; for to him who has this ornament, more adorning shall be given. He has promised that He will "beautify the meek with salvation;" and if the garments of salvation will not beautify, what will? The robes of glory will be the everlasting ornaments of meek and quiet spirits. This meekness is an ornament that, like the Israelites' clothes in the wilderness, never grows old, nor will ever go out of fashion while right reason and religion have place in the world: all the wise and good will consider those best dressed that put on the Lord Jesus Christ, and walk with Him in the white of meekness and innocency. Solomon in all his glory was not arrayed like one of these lilies of the valleys, though lilies among thorns.

The same ornament which is recommended to wives, is by the same apostle recommended to us all. "Yes, all of you be subject one to another:" that explains what meekness is; it is that mutual yielding which we owe one to another, for edification and in the fear of God. This seems to be a hard saying; how shall we digest it? an impracticable duty; how shall we conquer it? Why, it follows, "Be clothed with humility." Which implies, 1. the fixedness of this grace: we must gird it fast to us, and not leave it to hang loose, so as to be snatched away by every temptation: watchfulness and resolution in the strength of Christ must tie the knot upon our graces, and make them as the belt that cleaves to a man's loins. 2. The loveliness and ornament of it; put it on as a knot of ribbons, as an ornament to the soul: such is the meekness of wisdom; it gives to the head an ornament of grace, and, which is more, a crown of glory. Prov. 1:9; 6:9.

4. There is in it the credit of true courage. Meekness is commonly despised by the noblemen of the age as cowardice and lowliness, and the evidence of a little soul, and is posted accordingly; while the most furious and angry revenge is celebrated and applauded under the pompous names of valor, honor, and greatness of spirit. This arises from a mistaken notion of courage, the true nature whereof is thus stated by a very ingenious pen: "It is a resolution never to decline any evil of pain, when the choosing of it, and the exposing of ourselves to it, is the only remedy against a greater evil." And therefore he that accepts a challenge, and so runs himself upon the evil of sin, which is the greater evil, only for fear of shame and reproach, which is the less evil, is the coward; while he that refuses the challenge, and so exposes himself to reproach for fear of sin,* he is the valiant man. True courage is such a presence of mind as enables a man rather to suffer than to sin; to choose affliction rather than iniquity; to pass by an affront though he lose by it, and be hissed as a fool and a coward,

rather than engage in a sinful quarrel. He that can deny the brutal lust of anger and revenge, rather than violate the royal law of love and charity, however contrary the sentiments of the world may be, is truly resolute and courageous; the Lord is with you, you mighty man of valor. Fretting and vexing is the fruit of the weakness of women and children, but much below the strength of a man, especially of the new man that is born from above. When our Lord Jesus is described in his majesty, riding prosperously, the glory in which He appears is "truth and meekness and righteousness." The courage of those who overcome this great red dragon of wrath and revenge by meek and patient suffering, and by not loving "their lives unto the death," will turn to the best and most honorable account on the other side the grave, and will be crowned with glory and honor and immortality, when those that caused their terror in the land of the living fall ingloriously, and bear their shame with those who go down to the pit. Ezek. 32:24.

*Paul showed more true valor when he said, I can do nothing against the truth, than Goliath did when he defied all the host of Israel. Ward.

It has the credit of a conformity to the best patterns. The resemblance of those that are confessedly excellent and glorious, has in it an excellence and glory. To be meek is to be like the greatest saints, the elders that obtained a good report, and were of renown in their generation. It is to be like the angels, whose meekness in their converse with, and ministration to the saints, is very observable in the Scriptures; more so, it is to be like the great God Himself, whose goodness is His glory, who is "slow to anger," and in whom "fury is not." We are then followers of God, as dear children, when we "walk in love," and are kind one to another, tender hearted, forgiving one another. The more quiet and sedate we are, the more like we are to that God who, though He is nearly concerned in all the affairs of this lower world, is far from being moved by its convulsions and revolutions; but, as He was from eternity, so He is, and will be to eternity, infinitely happy in the enjoyment of Himself. It is spoken to His praise and glory, The Lord sits upon the floods, even when the floods have lifted up their voices, have lifted up their waves. Such is the rest of the eternal Mind, that He sits as firm and undisturbed upon the movable flood as upon the immovable rock, the same yesterday, today, and forever; and the meek and quiet soul that preserves its peace and evenness against all the ruffling insults of passion and provocation, does thereby somewhat participate of a divine nature. 2 Pet. 1:4.

Let the true honor that attends this grace of meekness recommend it to us: it is one of those things that are honest and pure and lovely and of good report; a virtue that has a praise attending it—a praise not perhaps of men, but of God. It is the certain way to get and keep, if not a great name, yet a good name; such as is better than precious ointment. Though there are those that trample upon the meek of the earth, and look upon them as Michal upon David, despising them in their hearts; yet if this is to be vile, let us be yet more vile and base in our own might, and we shall find, as David argues, that there are those of whom we shall be "had in honor;" for the word of Christ shall not fall to the ground, that they "who humble themselves shall be exalted."

II. Consider how COMFORTABLE a meek and quiet spirit is. What is true comfort and pleasure but a quietness in our own bosom? Those are most easy to themselves who are so to all about them; while those who are a burden and a terror to others, will not be much otherwise to themselves. He that would lead a quiet, must lead "a peaceable life." The surest way to find rest to our souls is to "learn of Him who is meek and lowly in heart." Let but our moderation be known unto all men, and "the peace of God, which passes all understanding, will keep our hearts and minds." Quietness is the thing which even the busy, noisy part of the world pretend to desire and pursue: they will be quiet—this is their claim—yes, that they will, or they will know why; they will not endure the least disturbance of their quietness. But truly they go a mad way to work in pursuit of quietness; greatly to disquiet themselves inwardly, and put their souls into a continual tumult, only to prevent or remedy some small outward disquietude from others. But he that is meek finds a sweeter, safer quietness, and much greater comfort than that which they in vain pursue. "Great peace have they" that love this law of love, for "nothing shall offend them." Whatever offense is intended, it is not so interpreted, and by that means peace is preserved. If there is a heaven anywhere upon earth, it is in the meek and quiet soul that acts and breathes above that lower region which is infested with storms and tempests, the harmony of whose faculties is like the famed "music of the spheres"—a perpetual melody. "Mercy and truth are met together; righteousness and peace have kissed each other."

A meek and quiet Christian lives very comfortably, for he enjoys himself, he enjoys his friends, he enjoys his God, and he puts it out of the reach of his enemies to disturb him in these enjoyments.

1. He enjoys himself. Meekness is very closely related to that "patience" which our Lord Jesus prescribes to us as necessary to the keeping possession of our own souls. How

calm are the thoughts, how serene are the affections, how rational the prospects, and how even and composed are all the resolves of the meek and quiet soul! How free from the pains and tortures of an angry man, who is deprived and dispossessed even of himself, and while he toils and vexes to make other things his own, makes his own soul not so: his reason is in a mist; confounded and bewildered, it cannot argue, infer, or foresee with any certainty. His affections are on the full speed, hurried on with an impetus which is as uneasy as it is hazardous. Who is that "good man who is satisfied from himself?" Who but the quiet man that has no need to go abroad for satisfaction, but having Christ dwelling in his heart by faith, has in Him that peace which the world can neither give nor take away. While those that are fretful and passionate rise up early and sit up late, and eat the bread of sorrow in pursuit of revengeful projects, the God of peace gives to "his beloved sleep." The sleep of the meek is quiet and sweet and undisturbed; those that by innocence and mildness are the sheep of Christ, shall be made to "lie down in green pastures." That which would break an angry man's heart will not break a meek man's sleep. It is promised that "the meek shall eat and be satisfied." He has what sweetness is to be had in his common comforts; while the angry man either cannot eat, his stomach is too full and too high, as Ahab, 1 Kings 21:4, or eats and is not satisfied, unless he can be revenged, as Haman: "All this avails me nothing," though it was a banquet of wine with the king and queen, "as long as Mordecai is unhanged."

It is spoken of as the happiness of the meek, that they "delight themselves in the abundance of peace;" others may delight themselves in the abundance of wealth, a poor delight, that is interwoven with so much trouble and disquietude; but the meek, though they have but a little wealth, have peace, abundance of peace, peace like a river, and this such as they have a heart to enjoy. They have light within: as Oecolampadius said, Their souls are a Goshen in the midst of the Egypt of this world; they have a light in their dwelling when clouds and darkness are round about them: this is the joy with which a stranger does not intermeddle. We may certainly have—and we should do well to consider it—less inward disturbance, and more true ease and satisfaction, in forgiving twenty injuries than in avenging one. No doubt Abigail intended more than she expressed, when, to persuade David to pass by the affront which Nabal had given him, she prudently suggested that hereafter "this shall be no grief to you, nor offense of heart"—not only so, but it would be very sweet and easy and comfortable in the reflection. Such a rejoicing is it, especially in a suffering day, to have the testimony of conscience, that in simplicity and godly sincerity, not with fleshly wisdom, but by the grace of God, particularly the grace of meekness, we have had our conversation in the world, and so have pleased God and done our duty. He did not speak the sense, no, not of the sober heathen, that said, "Revenge is sweeter than life;" for it often proves more bitter than death.

2. He enjoys his friends; and that is a thing in which lies much of the comfort of human life. Man was intended to be a sociable creature, and a Christian much more so. But the angry man is unfit to be so, that takes fire at every provocation; fitter to be abandoned to the lions' dens and mountains of the leopards, than to go forth by the footsteps of the flock. He that has his hand against every man, cannot but have, with Ishmael's character, Ishmael's fate, "every man's hand against him," and so he lives in a state of war; but meekness is the cement of society, the bond of Christian communion: it planes and polishes the materials

of that beautiful fabric, and makes them lie close and tight, and the living stones which are built up a spiritual house, to be like the stones of the temple that Herod built, all as one stone, whereas, "Hard upon hard," as the Spaniard's proverb is, "will never make a wall." Meekness preserves among brethren that unity which is like the ointment upon the holy head, and the dew upon the holy hill. Psa. 133:1, 2. In our present state of imperfection, there can be no friendship, correspondence, or conversation maintained without mutual allowances; we do not yet dwell with angels or spirits of just men made perfect, but with men subject to like passions. Now meekness teaches us to consider this, and to allow accordingly; and so distance and strangeness, feuds and quarrels are happily prevented, and the beginnings of them crushed by a timely care. How necessary to true friendship it is to surrender our passions, and to subject them all to the laws of it, was perhaps intimated by Jonathan's delivering to David his sword and his bow and his belt, all his military habiliments, when he entered in a covenant with him.

3. He enjoys his God; and that is most comfortable of all. It is the quintessence of all happiness, and that without which all our other enjoyments are insipid; for this none are better qualified than those who are arrayed with the ornament of a meek and quiet spirit, which is in the sight of God of great price. It was when the psalmist had newly conquered an unruly passion and composed himself, that he lifted up his soul to God in that pious and emotional breathing, "Whom have I in heaven but You? and there is none upon earth that I desire besides You." We enjoy God when we have the evidences and the assurances of his favor, the tastes and tokens of his love—when we experience in ourselves the communication of his grace, and the continued instances of his image stamped upon us;

and this those that are most meek and quiet have usually in the greatest degree. In our wrath and passion we give place to the devil, and so provoke God to withdraw from us. Nothing grieves the Holy Spirit of God, by whom we have fellowship with the Father, more than "bitterness and wrath and anger and clamor and evil-speaking." But to this man does the God of heaven look with a particular regard, even to him that is poor, poor in spirit, Isa. 66:2: to him that is quiet, so the Syriac—to him that is meek, so the Chaldee. The great God overlooks heaven and earth to give a favorable look to the meek and quiet soul. Yes, He not only looks at such, but He "dwells" with them; noting a constant communion and communion between God and humble souls. His secret is with them; He gives them more grace; and those who thus dwell in love, dwell in God, and God in them. The waters were dark indeed, but they were quiet when the Spirit of God moved upon them, and out of them produced a beautiful world.

This calm and composed frame very much qualifies and disposes us for the reception and entertainment of divine visits; sets bounds to the mountain on which God is to descend, Exod. 19:12, that no interruption may break in; and charges the daughters of Jerusalem, by the roes and the hinds of the field—those sweet and gentle and peaceable creatures—not to stir up or awake our love until he please. Song 2:7. Some think it was for the quieting and composing of his spirit, which seems to have been a little ruffled, that Elisha called for the "musician," and then "the hand of the Lord came upon him." Never was God more intimate with any mere man than He was with Moses, the meekest of all the men on the earth; and it was required as a necessary qualification of the high priest, who was to draw near to minister, that he should have compassion on the ignorant, and on those who are out of the way. "The meek will He guide in judgment" with a still small voice, which cannot be heard when the passions are loud and tumultuous. The angry man when he awakes is still with the devil, devising some malicious project; the meek and quiet man when he awakes is still with God, solacing himself in his favor. "Return unto your rest, O my soul," says David, when he had reckoned himself among the simple, that is, the mild, innocent, and inoffensive people. Return to your Noah, so the word is—for Noah had his name from rest—perhaps alluding to the rest which the dove found with Noah in the ark, when she could find none anywhere else. Those that are harmless and simple as doves, can with comfort return to God as to their rest. It is excellently paraphrased by Mr. Patrick, "God and yourself," my soul, "enjoy; in quiet rest, freed from your fears." It is said that "the Lord lifts up the meek;" as far as their meekness reigns they are lifted up above the stormy region, and fixed in a sphere perpetually calm and serene. They are advanced indeed that are at home in God, and live a life of communion with Him, not only in solemn ordinances, but even in the common accidents and occurrences of the world. Every day is a Sabbath-day, a day of holy rest with the meek and quiet soul, as one of the days of heaven. As this grace becomes established, the comforts of the Holy Spirit grow stronger and stronger, according to that precious promise, "The meek also shall increase their joy in the Lord, and the poor among men shall rejoice in the Holy One of Israel."

4. It is not in the power of his enemies to disturb and interrupt him in these enjoyments. His peace is not only sweet but safe and secure; as far as he acts under the law of meekness, it is above the reach of the assaults of those that wish ill to it. He that abides quietly under "the shadow of the Almighty" shall surely be delivered "from the snare of

the fowler." The greatest provocations that men can give would not hurt us if we did not, by our inordinate and foolish concern, come too near them. We may therefore thank ourselves if we are damaged. He that has learned with meekness and quietness to forgive injuries and pass them by, has found the best and surest way of baffling and defeating them; more than that, it is a kind of innocent revenge. It was an evidence that Saul was actuated by another spirit, in that, when children of Belial despised him and brought him no presents—hoping by that contempt to give a shock to his infant government—he "held his peace," and so neither his soul nor his crown received any disturbance. Shimei, when he cursed David, intended thereby to pour vinegar into his wounds, and to add affliction to the afflicted; but David, by his meekness, preserved his peace, and Shimei's design was frustrated. "So let him curse;" alas, poor creature, he hurts himself more than David, who, while he keeps his heart from being tinder to those sparks, is no more prejudiced by them than the moon is by the foolish cur that barks at it. The meek man's prayer is that of David, "Lead me to the rock that is higher than I," Psa. 61:2; and there I can, as Mr. Norris expresses it,

    —smile to see
The shafts of fortune all drop short of me.

The meek man is like a ship that rides at anchor—is moved, but not removed: the storm moves it—the meek man is not a stock or stone under provocation—but does not remove it from its port. It is a grace that, in reference to the temptations of affront and injury—as faith in reference to temptation in general—quenches the fiery darts of the wicked: it is an armor of proof against the spiteful and poisonous arrows of provocation, and is an impenetrable wall to secure the peace of the soul, where no thief can break through to steal; while the angry man lays all his comforts at the mercy of every wasp that will strike at him.

So that, upon the whole, it appears that the ornament of a meek and quiet spirit is as easy as it is attractive.

III. Consider how PROFITABLE a meek and quiet spirit is. All are intent on gain. It is for this that they lose sleep and spend their spirits. Now it will be hard to convince such, that really there is more to be obtained by meekness and quietness of spirit, than by all this tumult and confusion. They readily believe that "in all labor there is profit:" but let God Himself tell them, "In returning and rest you shall be saved; in quietness and in confidence shall be your strength;" they will not take His word for it, but they say, "No; for we will flee upon horses, and we will ride upon the swift." He that came from heaven to bless us has entailed a special blessing upon the grace of meekness: "Blessed are the meek;" and His saying they are blessed makes them so; for those whom He blesses are blessed indeed—blessed, and they shall be blessed. Meekness is gainful and profitable, as it is,

1. The condition of the promise: the meek "shall inherit the earth:" it is quoted from Psa. 37:11, and is almost the only express promise of temporal good things in all the New Testament. Not that the meek shall be put off with the earth only, then they would not be truly blessed; but they shall have that as an earnest of something more. Some read it, They shall inherit the land, that is, the land of Canaan, which was not only a type and figure, but to those who believed, a token and pledge of the heavenly inheritance. So that "a double Canaan," as Dr. Hammond observes, "is thought little enough for the meek man; the same felicity in a manner attending him which we believe

of Adam, if he had not fallen—a life in paradise, and then a transplantation to heaven." Meekness is a branch of godliness which has, more than other branches of it, "the promise of the life that now is." They shall inherit the earth; the sweetest and surest tenure is that by inheritance, which is founded in sonship: that which comes by descent to the heir, the law attributes to the act of God, who has a special hand in providing for the meek. They are His children; and if children, then heirs. It is not always the largest proportion of this world's goods that falls to the meek man's share; but whether he has more or less, he has it by the best title—not by a common, but a covenant right: he holds in Capite, in Christ our head, an honorable tenure.*

*They inhabit the earth which they know to be theirs by the divine allotment, and they are safe beneath the divine protection; this suffices them until, in the last day, they arrive at the full possession of their inheritance. The furious, on the contrary, by grasping at all, lose everything. Calv. in Matthew 5:5

If he has but a little, he has it from God's love, and with His blessing, and behold all things are clean and comfortable to him. The wise man has determined it: "Better is a dry morsel with quietness, than a house full of feasting with strife. Better is a dinner of herbs where love is, than a fatter calf with hatred." Be the fare ever so meager, he that has rule over his own spirit, knows how to make the best of it, and how to suck honey out of the rock, and oil out of the flinty rock. Blessed are the meek; for they shall wield the earth: so old Wickliff's translation reads it— as I remember it is quoted in the Book of Martyrs—and very significantly. Good management contributes more to our comfort than great possessions. Whatever a meek man has of this earth, he knows how to wield it, to make a right and good use of it; that is all in all. Quiet souls so far inherit the earth that they are sure to have as much of it as is good for them, as much as will serve to bear their charges through this world to a better; and who would covet more? The promise of God without present possession, is better than possession of the world without an interest in the promise.

Meekness has in its own nature a direct tendency to our present benefit and advantage. He that is thus wise, is wise for himself even in this world, and effectually consults his own interest.

Meekness has a good influence upon our health. If envy is "the rottenness of the bones," meekness is the preservation of them. The excesses and exorbitances of anger stir up those bad humors in the body which kindle and increase wasting and killing diseases; but meekness governs those humors, and so contributes very much to the good temper and constitution of the body. When Ahab was sick for Naboth's vineyard, meekness would soon have cured him. Moses, the meekest of men, not only lived to be old, but was then free from the infirmities of age; "his eye was not dim, nor his natural force abated," which may be very much imputed to his meekness, as a means. The days of old age would not be such evil days if old people did not, by their own frowardness and unquietness, make them worse than otherwise they would be. Ungoverned anger inflames the natural heat, and so begets acute diseases— dries up the radical moisture, and so hastens chronic decays. The body is called the sheath or scabbard of the soul. Dan. 7:15, margin. How often does an envious, fretful soul, like a sharp knife, cut its own sheath, and as they say of the viper's brood, eat its own way out; all which meekness happily prevents.

The quietness of the spirit will help to suppress depression; and this, as other of wisdom's precepts, will be health to the body and marrow to the bones: length of days and long life and peace they shall add unto you; but wrath kills the foolish man. Job 5:2.

It has a good influence upon our wealth—the preservation and increase of it. As in kingdoms, so in families and neighborhoods, war begets poverty. Many a one has brought a fair estate to ruin by giving way to the efforts of an ungoverned anger, that savage idol, to which even the children's portions and the family's maintenance are oftentimes sacrificed. Contention will as soon clothe a man with rags as slothfulness; that therefore which keeps peace does not a little befriend plenty. It was Abraham's meek management of his quarrel with Lot that secured both his own and his kinsman's possessions, which otherwise would have been an easy prey to the Canaanite and the Perizzite that dwelt then in the land. And Isaac, whom I have sometimes thought to be the most quiet and calm of all the patriarchs, and that passed the days of his pilgrimage most silently, raised the greatest estate of any of them; he "grew until he became very great;" and his son Jacob lost nothing in the end by his meek and quiet carriage towards his uncle Laban. Revenge is costly. Haman bid largely for it, no less than ten thousand talents of silver. It is better to forgive, and save the charges. Mr. Dod used to say, "Love is better than law; for love is cheap, but law is chargeable." Those tradesmen are commonly observed to thrive most that make the least noise, that "with quietness work," and mind their own business.

It has a good influence upon our safety. In the day of the Lord's anger the meek of the earth are most likely to be secured. It may be you shall be hid—so runs the promise,

Zeph. 2:3—if any be, you shall; you stand fairest for special protection. Meekness approaches to that innocence which is commonly an effectual security against wrongs and injuries. However some base and servile spirits may exult over the tame and humble, yet with all people of honor it is confessedly a piece of cowardice to attack an unarmed, unresisting man that resents not provocation. "And who is he that will harm you, if you are followers of that which is good?" Who draws his sword or aims his pistol at the harmless silent lamb? while every one is ready to do it at the furious barking dog. Thus does the meek man escape many of those perplexing troubles, those woes and sorrows and wounds without cause, which he that is passionate, provoking, and revengeful pulls upon his own head. Wise men turn away wrath, but a fool's lips enter into contention, and his mouth calls for strokes. It is an honor to a man to cease from strife, but every fool will be meddling to his own hurt. An instance of this I remember Mr. Baxter gives in his book of "Obedient Patience:" "Once going along London streets, a hectoring, crude fellow jostled him; he went on his way, and took no notice of it; but the same man affronting the next he met in like manner, he drew his sword and demanded satisfaction, and mischief was done." He that would sleep, both in a whole skin and in a whole conscience, must learn rather to forgive injuries than to revenge them. The two goats that met upon the narrow bridge, as it is in Luther's fable, were both in danger should they quarrel; but were both preserved by the condescension of one that lay down and let the other go over him. It is the evil of passion, that it turns our friends into enemies; but it is the excellency of meekness, that it turns our enemies into friends, which is an effectual way of conquering them. Saul, as inveterate an enemy as could be, was more than once melted by David's mildness and meekness. "Is this your voice, my son David?" said he. "I have sinned: return, my son David." And after that Saul persecuted him no more. 1 Sam. 27:4. The change that Jacob's meekness made in Esau is no less observable. In the ordinary dispensations of Providence, some tell us that they have found it remarkably true in times of public trouble and calamity, that it has commonly fared best with the meek and quiet; their lot has been safe and easy, especially if compared with the contrary fate of the turbulent and rebellious. Whoever is wise and observes these things will understand the loving-kindness of the Lord to the quiet in the land, against whom we read indeed of plots laid and deceitful matters devised, Psa. 35:20; 37:12, 14; but those by a kind and overruling Providence are ordinarily baffled and made unsuccessful. Thus does this grace of meekness carry its own recompense along with it, and in keeping this commandment, as well as after keeping it, "there is a great reward."

IV. Consider what a PREPARATIVE it is for something further. It is a very desirable thing to stand complete in all the will of God, Col. 4:12, to be fitted and furnished for every good work, to be made ready, a people prepared for the Lord. A living principle of grace is the best preparation for the whole will of God. Grace is establishing to the heart, it is the root of the matter, and a good foundation for the time to come. This grace of meekness is particularly a good preparation for what lies before us in this world.

1. It makes us fit for any duty. It puts the soul in frame, and keeps it so for all religious exercises. There was no noise of axes and hammers in the building of the temple: those are most fit for temple service that are most quiet and composed. The work of God is best done when it is done without noise.

Meekness qualifies and disposes us to hear and receive the word: when malice and envy are laid aside, and we are like newborn babies for innocence and inoffensiveness, then we are most fit to receive the sincere milk of the word, and are most likely to grow thereby. Meekness prepares the soil of the heart for the seed of the word, as the husbandman opens and breaks the clods of his ground, and makes plain the face thereof, and then casts in "the principal wheat and the appointed barley." Christ's ministers are fishers of men, but we seldom fish successfully in these troubled waters. The voice that Eliphaz heard was ushered in with a profound silence, and in slumberings upon the bed—a quiet place and posture. God "opens the ears of men, and seals their instructions."

Prayer is another duty which meekness disposes us rightly and acceptably to perform. We do not lift up pure hands in prayer, if they are not "without wrath." Prayers made in wrath are written in gall, and can never be pleasing to, or prevailing with the God of love and peace. Our rule is, "First go and be reconciled to your brother, and then come and offer your gift." And if we do not take this method, though we seek God in a due ordinance, we do not seek Him in the due order.

The Lord's day is a day of rest, and none are fit for it but those who are in a quiet frame, whose souls have entered into that present sabbatism which the gospel has provided for the people of God. The Lord's supper is the gospel-feast of unleavened bread, which must be kept, not with the old leaven of wrath and malice and wickedness, but with the unleavened bread of sincerity and truth.*

* How can we attain the peace of God without peace? How can we attain the remission of our sins without

remitting the sins of others? How can he that is angry with his brother pacify his Father, who, from the first, forbids us to be angry? Turtel. de Orat. c. 10

God made a gracious visit to Abraham, and after that the strife between him and Lot was over, in which he had discovered so much mildness and humility. The more carefully we preserve the communion of saints, the fatter we are for communion with God. It is observable, that the sacrifices which God appointed under the law, were not ravenous beasts and birds of prey, but calves and kids and lambs and turtle-doves and young pigeons, all of them emblems of meekness and gentleness and inoffensiveness; for with such sacrifices God is well pleased. This quietness of spirit contributes very much to the constant steadiness and regularity of a religious conversation. Hot and eager spirits, that are ready to take fire at every thing, are usually very inconsistent in their profession, and of great inconsistency with themselves: like a man with a fever, sometimes burning with heat, and sometimes shivering with cold; or like those that gallop in the beginning of their journey, and tire before the end of it; whereas the meek and quiet Christian is still the same, and by keeping to a constant rate, makes progress. If you would have one foot of the compass go even round the circumference, you must be sure to keep the other fixed and quiet in the center, for your strength is to sit still.

2. It makes us fit for any relation into which God in His providence may call us. Those who are quiet themselves, cannot but be easy to all that are about them; and the nearer any are to us in relation and conversation, the more desirable it is that we should be easy to them. Relations are various, as superiors, inferiors, and equals; he that is of a meek and quiet spirit is fitted for any of them.

Moses was forty years a courtier in Egypt, forty years a
servant in Midian, and forty years a king in Jeshurun; and
his meekness qualified him for each of these posts, and still
he held fast his integrity. Various duties are required
according to the relationship, and various graces to be
exercised; but this grace of meekness is the golden thread
that must run through all. If man is a sociable creature, the
more he has of humanity, the more fit he is for society.
Meekness would greatly help to preserve the wisdom and
due authority of superiors, the obedience and due
subjection of inferiors, and the love and mutual kindness of
equals. A calm and quiet spirit receives the comfort of the
relationship most thankfully, studies the duty of the
relationship most carefully, and bears the inconvenience of
the relationship—for there is no unmixed comfort under the
sun—most cheerfully and easily. I have heard of a married
couple, who, though they were both naturally of a quick
temper, yet lived very comfortably in that relationship by
observing an agreement made between themselves, "never
both to be angry together:" an excellent law of meekness,
which, if faithfully obeyed, would prevent many of those
breaches among relationships which occasion so much guilt
and grief, and are seldom healed without a scar. It was part
of the good advice given by a pious and ingenious father to
his children newly entered into the conjugal relation:

> Does one speak fire? t'other with water come;
> Is one provoked ? be t'oher soft or dumb.

And thus one wise, both happy. But where wrath and
anger are indulged, all relationships are embittered; those
that should be helps, become as thorns in our eyes and
goads in our sides. Two indeed are better than one, and yet
it is better to dwell alone in the wilderness, than with a

contentious and angry relative, who is like "a continual dropping in a very rainy day."

3. It makes us fit for any condition, according as the wise God shall please to dispose of us. Those who, through grace, are enabled to compose and quiet themselves, are fit to live in this world, where we meet with so much every day to disturb and disquiet us. In general, whether the outward condition is prosperous or adverse, whether the world smiles or frowns upon us, a meek and quiet spirit is neither lifted up with the one nor cast down with the other, but is still in the same poise: in prosperity humble and condescending, the estate rising, but the mind not rising with it; in adversity encouraged and cheered—cast down, but not in despair. St. Paul, who had learned in every estate "to be content, knew how to be abased, and knew how to abound;

everywhere, and in all things, he was instructed both to be full and to be hungry, both to abound and to suffer need." Changes without made none within. It is a temper which, as far as it has dominion in the soul, makes every burden light, by bringing the mind to the condition, when the condition is not in everything brought to the mind. Prosperity and adversity each have their particular temptation to peevishness and frowardness; the former by making men imperious, the latter by making them impatient. Against the assaults of each of these temptations the grace of meekness will stand upon the guard. Being to pass through this world "by honor and dishonor, by evil report and good report," that is, through a great variety of conditions and of treatment, we have need of that patience and kindness and love sincere which will be "the armor of righteousness on the right hand and on the left." Meekness and quietness will fortify the soul on each hand, and suit it to the several entertainments which the world gives us; like a skillful pilot that, from whatever point of the compass the wind blows, will shift his sails accordingly, and knows either how to get forward and weather his point with it, or to lie by without damage. It is the continual happiness of a quiet temper to make the best of that which is.*

*Seek not to adjust events to your will, so much as to adjust your will to events; thus you will act a becoming part. Epict. c. 13.

4. It makes us fit for a day of persecution. If tribulation and affliction arise because of the word—which is no foreign supposition—the meek and quiet spirit is armed for it, so as to preserve its peace and purity at such a time, which are our two great concerns, that we may neither torment ourselves with a base fear, nor pollute ourselves with a base compliance. We are used to saying, we "will give anything for a quiet life;" I say, anything for a quiet conscience, which will be best secured under the shield of a meek and quiet spirit, which does not "render railing for railing," nor aggravate the threatened trouble, nor represent it to itself in its most formidable colors, but has learned to put a but upon the power of the most enraged enemies; they can but kill the body; and to witness the most righteous testimony with meekness and fear, like our Master, who, "when He suffered, threatened not, but committed Himself to Him that judges righteously." Suffering saints—as the suffering Jesus—are compared to sheep dumb before the shearer, no, more than that, dumb before the butcher. The meek and quiet Christian, if duly called to it, can calmly part, not only with the wool, but with the blood; not only with the estate, but with the life, and even then rejoice with joy unspeakable and full of glory. Angry, contentious people, in a day of rebuke, are

apt to pull crosses upon themselves by needless provocations; or to murmur and complain, and fly in the face of instruments, and give unbecoming language, contrary to the laws of our holy religion and the example of our Master, and therefore get more hurt than good by their suffering. Whenever we have the honor to be persecuted for righteousness' sake, our great care must be to glorify God and to adorn our profession, which is done most effectually by meekness and mildness, under the hardest censures and the most cruel usage; so demonstrating that we are indeed under the power and influence of that holy religion for which we think it worth our while to suffer.

5. It makes us fit for death and eternity. The grave is a quiet place; "there the wicked cease from troubling." Those that were most troublesome are there bound to the peace; and "their hatred and envy" are there "perished." Whether we will or no, in the grave we shall lie still and be quiet. Job 3:13. What a great change then must it be to the unquiet, the angry and litigious; and what a mighty shock will that sudden, forced rest give them, after such a violent, rapid motion. It is therefore our wisdom to compose ourselves for the grave; to prepare ourselves for it, by adapting and accommodating ourselves to that which is likely to be our long home. This is dying daily, quieting ourselves, for death will shortly quiet us.

The meek and quiet soul is, at death, let into that rest which it has been so much laboring after; and how welcome must that be. Thoughts of death and the grave are very agreeable to those who love to be quiet; for then and there "they shall enter into peace," and "rest in their beds."

After death we expect the judgment, than which nothing is more dreadful to those who are "contentious."

The coming of the Master brings terror along with it to those who "smite their fellow-servants;" but those that are meek and quiet are likely to have their plea ready, their accounts stated, and whenever it comes it will be no surprise to them: to those whose "moderation is known to all men," it will be no ungrateful news to hear that "the Lord is at hand." It is therefore prescribed as that which ought to be our constant concern, that whenever our Master comes, we may "be found of Him in peace," that is, in a peaceable temper. Blessed is that servant whom His Lord when He comes shall find in such a frame. "A good man," says the late excellent Archbishop Tillotson, in his preface to his book of Family Religion, "would be loath to be taken out of the world reeking hot from a sharp contention with a perverse adversary; and not a little out of countenance to find himself in this temper translated into the calm and peaceable regions of the blessed, where nothing but perfect charity and goodwill reigns forever." Heaven is a quiet place, and none are fit for it but quiet people. The heavenly Canaan, that land of peace, would be no heaven to those that delight in war. The turbulent and unquiet would be out of their element, like a fish upon the dry ground, in those calm regions.

They are the sheep of Christ—such as are patient and inoffensive—that are called to inherit the kingdom; outside are dogs, that bite and devour. Rev. 22:15.

They are the wings of a dove, not those of a hawk or eagle, that David would fly upon to his desired rest. Psalm 55:6.

Now lay all this together, and then consider whether or not there is a real excellence in this meekness and quietness of spirit, which highly recommends it to all that love either God or themselves, or have any sensible regard to their own comfort, either in this world or in that which is to come.

LACK OF MEEKNESS LAMENTED

And now, have we not reason to lament the lack of the adornment of a meek and quiet spirit among those that profess religion, and especially in our own hearts? If this is Christianity, how little is there of the thing, even among those that make great pretensions to the name! Surely, as one said in another case, either this is not gospel, or these are not gospel-professors. And oh, how bare and unbecoming does profession appear for lack of this adorning! When the Israelites had stripped themselves of their ornaments to furnish up a golden calf, it is said they were "made naked to their shame." How naked are we—like Adam when he had sinned—for lack of this ornament. It is well if it be to the shame of true repentance.

I am not teaching you to judge and censure others in this matter; there is too much of that to be found among us: we are quick-sighted enough to spy faults in others, the transports of whose passions we should interpret favorably. But we have all cause, more or less, to condemn ourselves, and confess guilt in this matter. In many things we all offend, and perhaps in this as much as in any, coming short of the law of meekness and quietness.

We are called Christians, and it is our privilege and honor that we are so: we name the name of the meek and lowly Jesus, but how few are actuated by his spirit, or conform to His example! It is a shame that any occasion should be given to charge it upon professors, who, in other things, are most strict and sober, that in this they are most faulty; and that many who pretend to conscience and devotion, should indulge themselves in a peevish, contentious, and morose temper and conversation, to the great reproach of that worthy name by which we are called. May we not say, as that Mahommedan did when a Christian prince had perfidiously broke his league with him, "O Jesus, are these Your Christians?"

It is the manifest design of our holy and excellent religion to smooth and soften and sweeten our temper; and is it not a wretched thing that any who profess it should be soured and embittered, and less conversant and fit for human society than others? He was looked upon as a very good man in his day, and not without cause, who yet had such an unhappy temper, and was sometimes so transported with passion that his friend would say of him, "He had grace enough for ten men, and yet not enough for himself." The disciples of Jesus Christ did not know "what manner of spirit they were of," so apt are we to deceive ourselves, especially when these extravagances shroud themselves under the specious and plausible pretense of zeal for God and religion. But yet the fault is not to be laid upon the profession, or the strictness and singularity of it in other things which are praiseworthy; nor may we think the worse of Christianity for any such blemish: we know very well that the wisdom that is from above is peaceable and gentle, and easy to be entreated, and all that is sweet and amiable and endearing, though she is not herein justified of all who call themselves her children. But the blame must be laid upon the corruption and folly of the professors themselves, who are not so perfectly delivered into the mold of Christianity as they should be; but neglect their ornament, and prostitute their honor, and suffer the authority of their graces to be trampled upon. They let "fire go out of the rod of their branches, which devoured their fruit;" so that there is no meekness as a strong rod to be a scepter to rule in the soul, which is "a lamentation, and shall be for a lamentation."

And yet, blessed be God, even in this corrupt and degenerate world there are many who appear in the excellent ornament of a meek and quiet spirit; and some whose natural temper is quick and choleric, yet have been enabled, by the power of divine grace, to show in a good conversation their works with meekness and wisdom. It is not so impractical as some imagine to subdue these passions, and to preserve the peace of the soul, even in a stormy day.

But that we may each of us judge ourselves and find matter for repentance herein, I shall only mention those instances of irregular deportment towards our particular relations which evidence the lack of meekness and quietness of spirit.

1. Superiors are commonly very apt to chide, and that is for lack of meekness. It is spoken to the praise of Him who is the great ruler of this perverse and rebellious world, that He "will not always chide." But how many little rulers are there of families and petty societies that herein are very unlike Him, for they are always chiding. Upon every little default they are put into a flame, and transported beyond due bounds; easily provoked, either for no cause at all, or for very small cause; greatly provoked, and very outrageous and unreasonable when they are provoked. Their bearing is fiery and hasty, their language is scurrilous and indecent; they care not what they say, nor what they do, nor whom they insult; they are "such sons of Belial, that a man cannot speak to them." One had as good meet a bear robbed of her whelps as meet them. These require meekness. Husbands should not be bitter against their wives. Parents should not provoke their children. Masters must forbear threatening. These are the rules, but how few are ruled by them. The undue and intemperate passion of

superiors goes under the excuse of necessary strictness and the maintaining of authority, and the education and control of children and servants. But surely every little failure need not be criticized, but rather should be passed by; or if the fault must be reproved and corrected, may it not be done without so much noise and clamor? Is this the product of a meek and quiet spirit? Is this the best badge of your authority you have to put on? And are these the ensigns of your honor? Is there no other way of making your inferiors know their place but by putting them among the dogs of your flock, and threatening them as such? Not that I am against government and good order in families, and such reproofs as are necessary to the support and preservation of it, and those so sharpened as some tempers require and call for. But while you are governing others, please learn to govern yourselves, and do not disorder your own souls under pretense of keeping order in your families; for though you yourselves may not be aware of it, yet it is certain that by those indications of your displeasure which transgress the laws of meekness, you do but render yourselves contemptible and ridiculous, and rather prostitute than preserve your authority. Though your children dare not tell you so, yet perhaps they cannot but think that you are very unfit to command yourselves.* Time was when you were yourselves children and scholars, and perhaps servants and apprentices; and so, if you will but allow yourselves the liberty of reflection, you cannot but know the heart of an inferior, Exod. 23:9, and should therefore treat those that are now under you as you yourselves then wished to be treated. A due expression of displeasure, so much as is necessary to the amendment of what is amiss, will very well consist with meekness and quietness. And your gravity and dreadful composure therein will contribute very much to the preserving of your authority, and will command respect abundantly more than your noise and scolding. Masters of families and masters of schools too have need, in this matter, to behave themselves wisely, so as to avoid the two extremes, that of Eli's foolish indulgence on the one hand, and that of Saul's brutish rage on the other; and for attaining this golden mean, wisdom is profitable to direct.

*No one is fit to rule except he is willing to be governed. Seneca.

2. Inferiors are commonly very apt to complain. If everything is not fair to their mind, they are fretting and vexing, and their hearts are hot within them; they are uneasy in their place and station, finding fault with everything that is said or done to them. Here is lacking a quiet spirit, which would reconcile us to the post we are in, and to all the difficulties of it, and would make the best of the present state, though it is attended with many inconveniences. Those unquiet people whom the apostle Jude in his epistle compares to raging waves of the sea and wandering stars, were murmurers and complainers— blamers of their lot, so the word signifies. It is an instance of unquietness, to be ever and anon quarreling with our allotment. Those wives lacked a meek and quiet spirit who "covered the altar of the Lord with tears:" not tears of repentance for sin, but tears of vexation at the disappointments they met in their outward condition. Hannah's meekness and quietness was in some degree lacking, when she fretted and wept, and would not eat; but prayer composed her spirit; her countenance was no more sad. It was the unquietness of the spirit of the elder brother in the parable, that quarreled so unreasonably with his father for receiving and entertaining the penitent prodigal. Those that are given to be uneasy, will never lack something or other to complain of. It is true, though not so

readily apprehended, that the sullenness and murmuring and silent frets of children and servants, are as great a transgression of the law of meekness, as the more open, noisy, and avowed passions of their parents and masters. We find the king's chamberlains angry with the king. And Cain's quarrel with God Himself for accepting Abel, was interpreted as anger by God. "Why are you angry, and why is your countenance fallen?" The sour looks of inferiors are as certain indicators of anger resting in the bosom, as the disdainful looks of superiors; and how many such instances of discontentment there have been, especially under a continual cross, our own consciences may perhaps tell us. It is the lack of meekness only that makes those whom divine Providence has put under the yoke, children of Belial, that is, impatient of the yoke.

3. Equals are commonly very apt to clash and contend. It is for lack of meekness that there are in the church so many pulpit and paper quarrels, such strifes of words and perverse disputings; that there are in the state such factions and parties, and between them such animosities and heart-burnings; that there are in neighborhoods such strifes and brawls and vexatious lawsuits, or such distances and estrangements and shyness one of another; that there are in families envies and quarrels among the children and servants, crossing, thwarting, and finding fault one with another; and that brethren that dwell together do not, as they should, dwell together in unity. It is for lack of meekness that we are so impatient of contradiction in our opinions, desires, and designs, that we must have our own saying, right or wrong, and everything our own way; that we are so impatient of competitors, not enduring that any should stand in our light, or share in that work of honor which we would engross to ourselves; that we are so impatient of contempt, so quick in our apprehension and

resentment of the least slight of affront, and so pregnant in our fancy of injuries, where really there are none, or none intended. They are not only loud and professed contentions that evidence a lack of meekness, but also those silent alienations in affection and conversation which make a less noise; little piques and prejudices conceived, which men are themselves so ashamed of that they will not own them: these show the spirit disturbed, and lacking the ornament of meekness. In a word, willfully doing anything to disquiet others—slandering, backbiting, whispering, talebearing, or the like, is too plain an evidence that we are not ourselves rightly disposed to be quiet.

And now, may we not all remember our faults this day; and instead of condemning others, though ever so faulty, should we not each of us bewail before the Lord that we have been so little motivated by this excellent spirit, and repent of all we have at any time said or done contrary to the law of meekness? Instead of going about to extenuate and excuse our sinful passions, let us rather aggravate them, and lay a load upon ourselves for them: "So foolish have I been and ignorant, and so like a beast before God." Think how often we have appeared before God, and the world without our ornament, without our livery, to our shame. God kept account of the particular instances of the unquietness of Israel: "They have tempted me," says He, "now these ten times." Conscience is God's register that records all our miscarriages: even what we say and do in our haste, is not so quick as to escape its observation. Let us therefore be often opening that book now, for our conviction and humiliation, or else it will be opened shortly to our confusion and condemnation. But if we would judge ourselves, we should not be judged of the Lord. May we not all say, as Joseph's brethren did—and perhaps some are, as they were, in a special manner called to say it by humbling providences—"We are verily guilty concerning our brother." Such a time, in such a company, upon such an occasion I lacked meekness; my spirit was provoked, and I spoke unadvisedly with my lips, and now I remember it against myself. More, have not I lived a life of unquietness in the family, in the neighborhood, always in the fire of contention, as in my element, and breathing threatenings? And by so doing have not I dishonored my God, discredited my profession, disturbed my soul, grieved the blessed Spirit, and been to many an occasion of sin? And for all this should I not be greatly humbled and ashamed? Before we can put on the ornament of a meek and quiet spirit, we must wash in the laver of true repentance, not only for our gross and open extravagances of passion, but for all our neglects and omissions of the duties of meekness.

ENCOURAGEMENTS TO MEEKNESS—
SCRIPTURE PRECEPTS

Have we not reason to labor and endeavor, since there is such a virtue and such a praise, to attain these things? Should we not lay out ourselves to the utmost for this ornament of a meek and quiet spirit? For your direction in this endeavor, if you are indeed willing to be directed, I shall briefly lay before you some Scripture precepts concerning meekness; some patterns of it; some particular instances in which we have special need of it; some good principles that we should abide by; and some good practices that we should abound in, in order to our growth in this grace. In opening these things, we will endeavor to keep close to the law, and to the testimony.

If we lay the word of God before us for our rule, and will be ruled by it, we shall find the command of God making meekness and quietness as much our duty as they are our ornament. We are there told, as the will of God that we must seek meekness.

1. This command we have in Zeph. 2:3, and it is especially directed to the meek: "Seek the Lord, all you meek of the earth—seek meekness." Though they were meek, and were pronounced so by Him that searches the heart, yet they must seek meekness; which teaches us that those who have much of this grace, have still need of more, and must desire and endeavor after more. He that sits down content with the grace he has, and is not pressing forward towards perfection, and striving to grow in grace, to get the habit of it more strengthened and confirmed, and the operation of it more quickened and invigorated, it is to be feared has no true grace at all; and that, though he sits ever

so high and ever so easy in his own opinion, he will yet sit down short of heaven. Where there is life, one way or other there will be growth, until we come to the perfect man. "He that has clean hands shall be stronger and stronger." Paul was a man of great attainments in grace, and yet we find him "forgetting the things that are behind, and reaching forward to those that are ahead." Those who took joyfully the spoiling of their goods, are yet told that they "have need of patience." Thus the meek of the earth—who being on the earth, are in a state of infirmity and imperfection, of trial and temptation—have still need of meekness; that is, they must learn to be yet more calm and composed, more steady and even and regular in the government of their passions, and in the management of their whole conversation. They who have silenced all angry words, must learn to suppress the first risings and motions of angry thoughts.

It is observable that when the meek of the earth are especially concerned to seek meekness, when the day of the Lord's anger hastens on, when the times are bad, and desolating judgments are breaking in, then we have occasion for all the meekness we have and all we can get, and all is little enough: meekness towards God the author, and towards men the instruments of our trouble; meekness to bear the trial, and to bear our testimony in the trial. There is sometimes an "hour of temptation," a critical day when the exercise of meekness is the work of the day: sometimes the children of men are more than ordinarily provoking, and then the children of God have more than commonly need of meekness. When God is justly angry and men are unjustly angry, when our mother's children are angry with us and our Father angry too, there is anger enough stirring, and then "blessed are the meek," that are careful to keep possession of their souls when they can keep possession of nothing else.

Now the way prescribed for the attainment of meekness is to seek it. Ask it of God, pray for it: it is fruit of the Spirit, it is given by the God of all grace, and to Him we must go for it. It is a branch of that wisdom which he that lacks must ask of God, and it shall be given him. The God we address is called "the God of patience and consolation;" and He is the God of consolation because the God of patience—for the more patient we are, the more we are comforted under our afflictions—and as such we must look to Him when we come to Him for grace to make us "like-minded," that is, meek and loving one towards another, which is the apostle's errand at the throne of grace. God's people are, and should be, a generation that "covet the best gifts," and make their court to the best Giver, who never said to the wrestling seed of Jacob, Seek in vain; but has given us an assurance firm enough for us to build upon, and rich enough for us to encourage ourselves with—Seek, and you shall find. What would we more? Seek meekness, and you shall find it.

The promise annexed is very encouraging to the meek of the earth that seek meekness: "It may be you shall be hid in the day of the Lord's anger." Though it is but a promise with an "it may be," yet it ministers abundance of comfort: God's probabilities are better than the world's certainties; and the meek ones of the earth that hope in His mercy, and can venture their all upon an intimation of His good will, shall find to their comfort, that when God brings a flood upon the world of the ungodly, He has an ark for all his Noahs, His resting, quiet people, in which they shall be hid, it may be, from the calamity itself, at least from the sting and malignity of it—"HID," as Luther said, "either in heaven or under heaven, either in the possession or under the protection of heaven."

2. We must put on meekness. "Put on therefore, as the elect of God, holy and beloved, meekness." It is one of the members of the new man, which we must put on. Put it on as armor, to keep provocations from the heart, and so to defend the vitals. Those who have tried it will say it is "armor of proof." When you are putting on "the whole armor of God," do not forget this. Put it on as attire, as your necessary clothing, which you cannot go without; look upon yourselves as ungirt, undressed, unblessed without it. Put it on as a livery garment, by which you may be known to be the disciples of the meek and humble and patient Jesus, and to belong to that peaceable family. Put it on as an ornament, as a robe and a diadem, by which you may be both beautiful and dignified in the eyes of others. Put it on as the elect of God, holy and beloved, because you are so in profession; and that you may approve yourselves so in truth and reality, be clothed with meekness as the elect of God, a choice people, a chosen people, whom God has set apart for Himself from the rest of the world, as holy, sanctified to God, sanctified by Him: study these graces, which put such a luster upon holiness, and recommend it to those that are without, as beloved, beloved of God, beloved of man, beloved of your ministers: for love's sake, put on meekness. What winning, persuasive rhetoric is here! enough, one would think, to smooth the roughest soul, and to soften and sweeten the most obstinate heart. Meekness is a grace of the Spirit's working, a garment of his preparing; but we must put it on, that is, we must lay our souls under the commanding power and influence of it. Put it on, not as a loose outer garment, to be put off in hot weather, but let it cleave to us, as the belt cleaves to a man's loins; so put it on as to reckon ourselves naked to our shame without it.

3. We must follow after meekness. This precept we have, 1 Tim. 6:11. Meekness is there put in opposition to

those foolish and hurtful lusts that Timothy must flee from: "You, O man of God, flee these things, and follow after righteousness, godliness, faith, love, patience, meekness." See what good company it is ranked with. Every Christian is in a sense a man of God—though Timothy is called so as a minister—and those that belong to God are concerned to be and do so as to recommend themselves to Him, and His religion to the world; therefore let the men of God follow after meekness. The occasions and provocations of anger often set our meekness at a distance from us, and we have it to seek when we have most need of it; but we must follow after it, and not be taken off from the pursuit by any diversion whatever. While others are ingenious and industrious enough in following after malice and revenge, projecting and prosecuting angry designs, you be wise and diligent to preserve the peace both within doors and without. Following meekness bespeaks a sincere desire and a serious endeavor to get the mastery of our passion, and to check, govern, and moderate all the motions of it. Though we cannot fully attain this mastery, yet we must follow after it, and aim at it. Follow meekness, that is, as much as it is in you, live peacefully with all men, endeavoring to keep the unity of the spirit: we can only make one side of the bargain; if others will quarrel, yet let us be peaceful; if others will strike fire, that is their fault; let us not be as tinder to it.

4. We must show all meekness unto all men. This is one of the subjects which Paul directs a young minister to preach upon. "Put them in mind to show all meekness." It is that which we have need to be often reminded of. Meekness is there opposed to brawling and clamor, which is the fruit and product of our own anger, and the cause and provocation of the anger of others. Observe, it is "all meekness" that is here recommended to us, all kinds of

meekness—bearing meekness, and forbearing meekness; qualifying meekness, and condescending meekness; forgiving meekness; the meekness that endears our friends, and that which reconciles our enemies; the meekness of authority over inferiors; the meekness of obedience to superiors; and the meekness of wisdom towards all. "All meekness," is meekness in all relations, in reference to all injuries, all sorts of provocation, meekness in all the branches and instances of it: in this piece of our obedience we must be universal. Observe further, we must not only have meekness, all meekness, but we must show it by drawing out this grace into exercise as there is occasion: in our words, in our looks, in our actions, in every thing that falls under the observation of men, we must show that we have indeed a regard to the law of meekness, and that we make conscience of what we say and do when we are provoked. We must not only have the law of love written in our hearts, but on our tongues too we must have "the law of kindness." And thus the tree is known by its fruit. This light must shine, that others may see the good works of it, and hear the good works of it too, not to glorify us, but to glorify our Father; we should study to appear, in all our conversation, so mild and gentle and peaceful, that all who see us may witness for us that we are of the meek of the earth. We must not only be moderate, but "let our moderation be known."

He that is in this respect a wise man, let him show it in the "meekness of wisdom." What are good clothes worth if they are not worn? Why has the servant a fine livery given him, but to show it for the honor of his master, and of the family he belongs to? How can we say we are meek if we do not show it? The showing of our meekness will beautify our profession, and will adorn the doctrines of God our Savior, and may have a very good influence upon others, who cannot but be in love with such an excellent grace, when thus, like the ointment of the right hand, it betrays itself, and the house is filled with the odor of it.

Again, this meekness must be thus showed unto all men—foes as well as friends, those without as well as those within, all that we have anything to do with. We must show our meekness not only to those above us, of whom we stand in awe, but to those below us, over whom we have authority. The poor indeed use entreaties, but whatever is the practice, it is not the privilege of the rich to "answer roughly." We must show our meekness "not only to the good and gentle, but also to the contentious; for this is thank worthy." Our meekness must be as extensive as our love, so exceedingly broad is this commandment, "all meekness to all men." We must show this meekness most to those with whom we most converse. There are some that, when they are in company with strangers, appear very mild and good-humored, their behavior is plausible enough and complaisant; but in their families they are peevish and froward and ill-natured, and those about them hardly know how to speak to them: this shows that the fear of man gives greater check to their passion than the fear of God. Our rule is to be meek towards all, even to the brute creation, over whom we are lords, but must not be tyrants.

Observe the reason which the apostle gives why we should show all meekness towards all men; "for we ourselves also were sometimes foolish." Time was when perhaps we were as bad as the worst of those we are now angry at; and if now it is better with us, we are purely beholden to the free grace of God in Christ that made the difference; and shall we be harsh to our brethren, who have found God so kind to us? Has God forgiven us our great debt, and passed by so many willful provocations, and shall we be extreme to mark what is done amiss against us, and make the worst of every slip and oversight? The great gospel argument for mutual forbearance and forgiveness is, that "God for Christ's sake has forgiven us."

It may be of use also for the qualifying of our anger at inferiors, to remember not only our former sinfulness against God in our unconverted state, but our former infirmities in the age and state of inferiors: were not we ourselves sometimes foolish? Our children are careless and playful and froward, and scarcely governable; and were not we ourselves so when we were of their age? And if we have now put away childish things, yet they have not. Children may be brought up in the nurture and admonition of the Lord, without being provoked to wrath.

5. We must "study" to be quiet, that is, study not to disturb others, nor to be ourselves disturbed by others: be ambitious of this, as the greatest honor, so the word signifies. The most of men are ambitious of the honor of great business and power and preferment: they covet it, they court it, they compass sea and land to obtain it; but the ambition of a Christian should be carried out towards quietness: we should consider it the happiest post, and desire it accordingly, which lies most out of the road of provocation.

"Let him that will, ascend the tottering seat
Of courtly grandeur, and become as great
As are his mounting wishes: as for me,
Let sweet repose and rest my portion be.
————Let my age
Slide gently by, not overthwart the stage
Of public action, unheard, unseen,
And unconcerned, as if I never had been."

This is studying to be quiet. Subdue and keep under all those disorderly passions which tend to the disturbing and clouding of the soul. Compose yourselves to this holy rest; put yourselves in a posture to invite this blessed sleep which God gives to His beloved. Take pains, as students in arts and sciences do, to understand the mystery of this grace. I call it a mystery, because St. Paul, who was so well versed in the deep things of God, speaks of this as a mystery. "I am instructed," as in a mystery, "both to be full and to be hungry, both to abound and to suffer need:" that is, in one word, to be quiet. To study the are of quietness is to take pains with ourselves, to have in our own hearts the principles, rules, and laws of meekness; and to furnish ourselves with such considerations as tend to the quieting of the spirit in the midst of the greatest provocations. Others are studying to disquiet us; the more need we have to study how to quiet ourselves, by a careful watching against all that which is ruffling and discomposing. Christians should, above all studies, study to be quiet, and labor to be motivated by an even spirit under all the unevenness of Providence, and remember that one good word which Sir William Temple tells us the prince of Orange said he learned from the master of his ship, who, in a storm, was calling to the steersman, "Steady, steady." Let but the hand be steady and the heart quiet, and though our passage be rough, we may weather the point, and get safe to the harbor.

SCRIPTURE PATTERNS

Good examples help very much to illustrate and enforce good rules, bringing them closer to particular cases, and showing them to be practical. Precedents are of great use in the law. If we would be found walking in the same spirit, and walking in the same steps with those that are gone before us to glory, this is the spirit by which we must be motivated, and these the steps in which we must walk: this is the way of good men, for wise men to walk in. Let us go forth then "by the footsteps of the flock," and set ourselves to follow them who through faith and patience inherit the promises. We are surrounded by a great cloud of witnesses who will bear their testimony to the comfort of meekness, and upon trial recommend it to us; but we shall single out only some few from the Scripture.

1. Abraham was a pattern of meekness, and he was the father of the faithful. As he was famous for faith, so was he for meekness; for the more we have of faith towards God, the more we shall have of meekness towards all men. How meek was Abraham when there happened a strife between his herdsmen and Lot's, which, had it proceeded, might have been of ill consequence, for "the Canaanite and the Perizzite dwelled then in the land;" but it was seasonably overruled by the prudence of Abraham. "Let there be no strife, please:" though he might command peace, yet for love's sake he rather beseeches. Every word has an air of meekness, and a tendency to peace. And when the expedient for the prevention of strife was their parting from each other, though Lot was the junior, yet Abraham, for the sake of peace, quitted his right, and gave Lot the choice; and the gracious visit which God gave him thereupon was

an abundant recompense for his mildness and condescension.

Another instance of Abraham's meekness we have when Sarah quarreled with him so unreasonably about her maid, angry at that which she herself had done. "My wrong be upon you: the Lord judge between you and me." Abraham might soon have replied, You may thank yourself, it was your own contrivance; but laying aside the present provocation, he abides by one of the original rules of the relation, "Behold, your maid is in your hand." He did not answer passion with passion, that would have put all into a flame; but he answered passion with meekness, and so all was quiet.

Another instance of Abraham's meekness we have in the transactions between him and Abimelech his neighbor. He first enters into a covenant of friendship with him, which was confirmed by an oath, and then does not reproach him, but reproves him for a wrong that his servants had done him about a well of water; which gives us this rule of meekness, "Not to break friendship for a small matter of difference:" such and such occasions there are, which those who are disposed to it might quarrel about; but "what is that between me and you?"

If meekness rules, matters in variance may be fairly reasoned and adjusted without violation or infringement of friendship. This is the example of that great patriarch. The future happiness of the saints is represented as the bosom of Abraham—a quiet state. Those who hope to lie in the bosom of Abraham shortly, must tread in the steps of Abraham now, whose children we are as long as we thus do well, "and who," as Maimonides expresses it, "is the father of all who are gathered under the wings of the divine Majesty."

2. Moses was a pattern of meekness; it was his master-grace; that in which, more than in any other, he excelled. This testimony the Holy Spirit gives of him, that "the man Moses was very meek, above all the men which were upon the face of the earth."

This character of him is given upon occasion of an affront he received from those of his own house, which intimates that his quiet and patient bearing it, was the greatest proof and instance of his meekness. Those can bear any provocation that can bear it from their near relations. The meekness of Moses, as the patience of Job, was tried on all hands. Armor of proof shall be sure to be shot at. It should seem that his wife was none of the best-humored women; for what a passion was she in about the circumcising of her son, when she reproached him as a bloody husband; and we do not read of one word that he replied, but let her have her saying. When God was angry, and Zipporah angry, it was best for him to be quiet. The lot of his public work was cast "in the provocation, in the day of temptation in the wilderness;" but as if all the mutinies of murmuring Israel were too little to try the meekness of Moses, his own brother and sister, and those of no less a figure than Miriam the prophetess, and Aaron the saint of the Lord, quarrel with him, speak against him, envy his honor, reproach his marriage, and are ready to head a rebellion against him. God heard this, and was angry. Num. 12:2, 9; but Moses, though he had reason enough to resent it wrathfully, was not at all moved by it, took no notice of it, made no complaint to God, no answer to them, and we do not find one word that he said, until we find him praying heartily for his provoking sister, who was then under the tokens of God's displeasure for the affront she gave him. The less a man strives for himself, the more is God engaged in honor and faithfulness to appear for him. When Christ said, "I seek not mine own glory," he presently added, "but there is one that seeks and judges." And it was upon this occasion that Moses obtained this good report: "He was the meekest of all the men on the earth." "No man," says Bishop Hall, "could have given greater proofs of courage than Moses. He slew the Egyptian, beat the Midianite shepherds, confronted Pharaoh in his own court, not fearing the wrath of the king; he durst look God in the face amid all the terrors of mount Sinai, and draw near to the thick darkness where God was; and yet that Spirit which made and knew his heart, said he was the meekest, mildest man upon the earth. Mildness and fortitude may well lodge together in the same breast, which corrects the mistake of those that will allow none valiant but the fierce."

The meekness of Moses qualified him to be a magistrate, especially to be king in Jeshurun, among a people so very provoking that they gave him occasion to use all the meekness he had, and all little enough to bear their manners in the wilderness. When they murmured against him, quarreled with him, arraigned his authority, and were sometimes ready to stone him, he resented these provocations with very little of personal application or concern; but instead of using his interest in heaven to summon plagues upon them, he made it his business to stand in the gap, and by his intercession for them, to turn away the wrath of God from them; and this not once or twice only, but many times.

And yet we must observe that, though Moses was the meekest man in the world, yet when God's honor and glory were concerned, no one was more warm and zealous:

witness his resentment of the golden calf, when, in a holy indignation at that abominable iniquity, he deliberately broke the tables. And when Korah and his crew invaded the priest's office, Moses, in a pious wrath, said unto the Lord, "Do not respect their offering." He that was a lamb in his own cause, was a lion in the cause of God: anger at sin as sin is very well consistent with reigning meekness. Nor can it be forgotten that though Moses was eminent for meekness, yet he once transgressed the laws of it. When he was old, and his spirit was provoked, he spoke unadvisedly with his lips, and it went ill with him for it, Psa. 106:32; which is written not for imitation, but for admonition—not to justify our rash anger, but to engage us to stand on guard at all times against it, that he who thinks he stands may take heed lest he fall, and that he who has thus fallen may not wonder if he come under the rebukes of divine Providence for it in this world, as Moses did, and yet may not despair of being pardoned upon repentance.

3. David was a pattern of meekness, and it is promised that "the feeble shall be as David." In this, as in other instances, he was a man after God's own heart. When his own brother was so rough upon him without reason, "Why did you come down here?" how mild was his answer. "What have I done now? Is there not a cause?" When his enemies reproached him, he was not at all disturbed at it. "I, as a deaf man, heard not." When Saul persecuted him with such an unwearied malice, he did not take the advantage which Providence seemed to offer him, more than once, to revenge himself, but left it to God. David's meek spirit concurred with the proverb of the ancients: "Wickedness proceeds from the wicked, but my hand shall not be upon you." When Nabal's churlishness provoked him, yet Abigail's prudence soon pacified him, and it pleased him to be pacified. When Shimei cursed him with a

bitter curse in the day of his calamity, he resented not the offense, nor would hear any talk of punishing the offender: "So let him curse; let him alone, for the Lord has bidden him;" quietly committing his cause to God, who judges righteously. And other instances there are in his story which evidence the truth of what he said: "My soul is even like a weaned child." And yet David was a great soldier, a man of celebrated courage, that slew a lion and a bear, and a Philistine—as much a ravenous beast as either of them—which shows that it was his wisdom and grace, and not his cowardice, that at other times made him so quiet. David was a man that met with very many disquieting and disturbing events in the several scenes of his life, through which, though they sometimes ruffled him a little, yet, for the main, he preserved an admirable temper, and an evenness and composure of mind which was very exemplary. When, upon the surprise of a fright, he changed his behavior before Abimelech, and counterfeited that madness which angry people realize, yet his mind was so very quiet and undisturbed that at that time he penned the 34th Psalm, in which not only the excellency of the matter, and the calmness of the expression, but the composing of it alphabetically in the Hebrew—speaks him to be, even then, in a calm frame, and to have very much the command of his own thoughts. As at another time when his own followers spoke of stoning him, though he could not still the tumult of his troops, he could those of his spirit, for then he "encouraged himself in the Lord his God." As to those prayers against his enemies which we find in some of his psalms, surely they did not proceed from any such irregular passion as did in the least clash even with the evangelical laws of meekness. We cannot imagine that one who was so piously calm in his common conversation, should be sinfully hot in his devotion; nor are they to be looked upon as the private expressions of his own angry resentments, but as inspired predictions of God's judgments upon the public and obstinate enemies of Christ and His kingdom, as appears by comparing Psa. 69:22, 23, with Rom. 11:9, 10; and Psa. 109:8, with Acts 1:20. Nor are they any more opposite to the spirit of the gospel than the cries of the souls under the altar, or the triumphs of heaven and earth in the destruction of Babylon. Rev. 6:10; 19:1.

4. Paul was a pattern of meekness. Though his natural temper seems to have been warm and eager, which made him eminently active and zealous, yet that temper was so rectified and sanctified, that he was no less eminently meek: he became all things to all men. He studied to please all with whom he had to do, and to render himself engaging to them, for their good to edification. How patiently did he bear the greatest injuries and indignities, not only from Jews and heathens, but from false brethren, that were so very industrious to abuse and undermine him. How glad was he that Christ was preached, though out of envy and ill-will, by those that studied to add affliction to his bonds. In governing the church, he was not led by the sudden resolves of passion, but always deliberated calmly concerning the use of the rod of discipline when there was occasion for it. "Shall I come to you with a rod, or in the spirit of meekness?" that is, Shall I proceed immediately to censures, or shall I not rather continue the same gentle usage as hitherto, waiting still for your reformation? Here the spirit of meekness appears more open and legible than in the use of the rod, though that also is very well consistent with it.

Many other examples of meekness might be adduced, but the time would fail me to tell of Isaac and Jacob and Joseph and Joshua; of Samuel also, and Job and Jeremiah, and all the prophets and apostles, martyrs and confessors, and eminent saints, who by meekness subdued, not kingdoms, but their own spirits; stopped the mouths, not of lions, but of more fierce and formidable enemies; quenched the violence, not of fire, but of intemperate and more ungovernable passions; and so wrought righteousness, obtained promises, escaped the edge of the sword, and out of weakness were made strong; and by all this obtained a good report. Heb. 11:32-34. But, after all,

5. Our LORD JESUS was the great pattern of meekness and quietness of spirit; all the rest had their spots, but here is a copy without a blot. We must follow the rest no further than they were conformable to this great original: "Be followers of me," says Paul, "as I am of Christ." He fulfilled all righteousness, and was a complete example of all that is holy, just, and good; but I think in most, if not all those places of Scripture where He is particularly and expressly propounded to us for an example, it is to recommend to us some or other of the duties of Christianity; those, I mean, which tend to the sweetening of our conversation with one another. The Word was made flesh, and dwelt among us, that He might teach us how to dwell together in unity. We must walk in love, as Christ loved us; forgive, as Christ forgave us; please one another, for Christ pleased not Himself; be charitable to the poor, for we know the grace of our Lord Jesus; wash one another's feet, that is, stoop to the lowest offices of love, for Christ did so; doing all with lowliness of mind, for it is the same mind that was in Christ Jesus; but above all, our Lord Jesus was an example of meekness. Moses had this grace as a servant, but Christ as a son: He was anointed with it above measure. He is called the "Lamb of God," for His meekness and patience and inoffensiveness, and even in His exaltation He retains the same character. One of the elders told John that "the Lion

of the tribe of Judah" would open the sealed book; "and I beheld," says John, "and lo, a Lamb." He that was a lion for strength and courage, was a lamb for mildness and gentleness; and if a lion, yet "the Lion of the tribe of Judah," which the dying patriarch describes to be a lion gone up from the prey, and that is stooped down and couched, and not to be roused up, Gen. 49:9, indicating the quietness and repose even of this lion. If Christ is a lion, He is a lion resting: the devil is a lion roaring. But the adorations given to Christ by the heavenly hosts speak of Him as a Lamb. "Blessing and glory to Him that sits upon the throne;" they do not say, and to the Lion of the tribe of Judah, but the "the Lamb." Though He has a name given Him above every name, yet He will be known by that name which denotes His meekness, as if this were to be His name forever, and this his memorial to all generations. As He that rides upon the heavens by His name Jah, is the Father of the fatherless, and the Judge of the widows; so Christ rides "prosperously, because of meekness."

Now it is the character of all the saints that they follow the Lamb: as a lamb they follow Him in His meekness, and are therefore so often called the sheep of Christ. This is that part of his copy which He expressly calls us to write after: "Learn of me; for I am meek and lowly in heart." If the master is mild, it ill becomes the servant to be froward. The apostle is speaking of Christ's meekness under His sufferings, when he says that He "left us an example, that we should follow His steps."

Let us observe particularly the meekness of our Lord Jesus towards his Father, and towards his friends, and towards his foes, in each of which He is an example to us.

1. He was very meek toward God His Father, cheerfully submitting to His whole will, and standing complete in it. In His commanding will, "Lo, I come," says He, "I delight to do Your will:" though it enjoined Him a very hard service, yet it was "His food and drink;" and He always did those things that pleased His Father. So likewise in His disposing will He acquiesced from first to last. When He was entering on that sharp encounter, though sense startled at it, and said, "Father, if it be possible, let this cup pass from Me;" yet He soon submitted with a great deal of meekness: "Not as I will, but as You will." Though it was a very bitter cup, yet his Father put it into His hand, and therefore He drank it: "The cup that My Father has given Me, shall I not drink it?"

2. He was very meek towards His friends that loved and followed Him. With what remarkable instances of mildness, gentleness, and tenderness did He train up His disciples, though from first to last He was "a man of sorrows, and acquainted with grief." Where nature is corrupt, such are apt to be peevish and froward with those about them; yet how meekly and calmly did He bear with their weaknesses and infirmities. After they had been long under the inspection and influence of such a teacher, and had all the advantages that men could have for acquaintance with the things of God, yet how weak and defective were they in knowledge and gifts and graces! How ignorant and forgetful were they; how slow of heart to understand and believe! And what blunders did they make! Dull scholars it should seem they were, and bad proficients. But their hearts being upright with Him, He did not cast them off, nor turn them out of His school, but corrected their mistakes, instructed them in their duty and the doctrine they were to preach, by precept upon precept, and line upon line; and taught them, as they were able to bear it,

as one that considered their frame, and could "have compassion on the ignorant, and on those who are out of the way." As long as He was with them, so long He suffered them. Mark 9:19. This, as it is a great encouragement to Christian learners, so it is a great example to Christian teachers.

Also Christ was meek in his forgiving and passing by their unkindness and disrespect to Himself. He was not extreme to mark what they did amiss of this kind. When they murmured at the cost that was bestowed upon Him, and called it waste, and had indignation at it, He did not resent it as He might have done, nor seem to observe how much what they said reflected upon Him; nor did He condemn them any other way than by commending the woman. When Peter and James and John, the first three of His disciples, were with Him in the garden, and very unseasonably slept while He was in his agony praying, so little concerned did they seem to be for Him, yet observe how meekly He spoke to them: "Could you not watch with Me one hour?" And when they did not have a word to say for themselves, so inexcusable was their fault, He had something to say for them, and instead of accusing them, He apologizes for them: "The spirit indeed is willing, but the flesh is weak." When Peter had denied Him, and had cursed and sworn he did not know Him, than which— besides the falsehood and perfidiousness of it—nothing could be more unkind, with what meekness did He bear it! It is not said the Lord turned and frowned upon Peter, though he deserved to be frowned into hell, but "the Lord turned and looked upon Peter," and that look recovered him into the way to heaven: it was a kind look, and not an angry one. Some days after, when Christ and Peter met in Galilee, and had dined together as a token of reconciliation, and some discourse passed between them, not a word was said of this matter; Christ not upbraid him with his fault, nor chide him for it, nor did there appear any other fruit of the falling out of these lovers, but only the renewing of their love with greater endearments; which teaches us to forgive and forget the unkindness of those that are for the main our true friends, and if any occasion of difference happens, to turn it into an occasion of confirming our love to them.

3. He was very meek towards his enemies, that hated and persecuted Him. The whole story of His life is filled with instances of invincible meekness. While He "endured the contradiction of sinners against Himself," He had a perpetual serenity and harmony within, and was never in the least discomposed by it. When His preaching and miracles were caviled at and reproached, and He Himself represented under the blackest characters, not only as the drunkard's companion, but as the devil's confederate, with what a wonderful calmness did He bear it! How mildly did He answer with reason and tenderness, when He could have replied in thunder and lightning! How well satisfied, under all such invidious reflections, with this, that "wisdom is justified of all her children." When some of his disciples would have had fire from heaven upon those crude people that refused Him entertainment in their town, He was so far from complying with the motion, that He rebuked it: "You know not what manner of spirit you are of." "This persuasion does not come from Him who calls you." The design of Christ and of His holy religion is to shape men into a mild and merciful temper, and to make them sensibly tender of the lives and comfort even of their worst enemies. Christianity was intended to revive humanity, and to make those men, who had made themselves beasts. But our Lord Jesus did in a more especial manner evidence His meekness when He was in His last sufferings—that dreadful scene. Though He was the most innocent and the most excellent

person that ever was, who, by the doctrine He had preached and the miracles He had wrought, had richly deserved all the honors and respect that the world could pay Him, and infinitely more; and though the injuries He received were ingeniously and industriously contrived to the highest degree of affront and provocation; yet He bore all with an undisturbed meekness, and with that shield quenched all the fiery darts which his malicious enemies shot at Him.

His meekness towards His enemies appeared in what He said to them: not one angry word, in the midst of all the indignities they offered Him. "When He was reviled, He reviled not again." When He was buffeted and spit upon and abused, He took it all patiently; one would wonder at the gracious words which even then proceeded out of His mouth: witness that mild reply to him that smote him: "If I have spoken evil, bear witness of the evil; but if well, why do you strike Me?"

Also His meekness towards His enemies appeared in what He said to God for them: "Father, forgive them;" so giving an example to His own rule: "Pray for those who despitefully use you." Though He was then deeply engaged in the most solemn transaction that ever passed between heaven and earth, though He had so much to do with God for Himself and His friends, yet He did not forget to offer this prayer for His enemies.

The mercy He begged of God for them was the greatest mercy—that which He was then dying to purchase and procure—the pardon of their sins: not only, Father, spare them, or reprieve them, but, Father, forgive them; the excuse He pleaded for them was the best their crime was capable of: "They know not what they do."

Now in all these things our Master has left us an example. What is the practice of religion, but the imitation of God endeavored by us? And what is the principle of it, but the image of God renewed in us? We are bid to be followers of God, as dear children. But this sets the copy we are to write after at a mighty distance, for God is in heaven, and we are upon earth; and therefore in the Lord Jesus Christ, God incarnate, God in our nature, the copy is brought among us, and the transcribing of it in some measure appears more practicable. "He that has seen Me," says Christ, "has seen the Father;" and so he that imitates Christ, imitates the Father. The religion which our Lord Jesus came into the world to establish, being every way so well calculated for the peace and order of the world, and being designed to recover the lapsed souls of men from their degenerate state, and to sweeten their spirits and temper, and so to befriend human society, and to make it some way conformable to the blessed society above; He not only gave such precepts as were wonderfully fitted to this great end, but recommended them to the world by the loveliness and amiableness of His own example. Are we not called Christians from Christ, whom we call Master and Lord, and shall we not endeavor to accommodate ourselves to Him? We profess to rejoice in Him as our forerunner, and shall we not run after Him? To what purpose were we listed under His banner, but that we might follow Him as our leader? We all have reason to say that Jesus Christ is very meek, or else we that have provoked Him so much and so often would have been in hell long ago; we owe it to His meekness, to whom all judgment is committed, that we have not before this been carried away with a swift destruction, and dealt with according to the desert of our sins, which, if duly considered, one would think should tend greatly to soften us. The apostle draws an argument from that kindness and love to us which we ourselves have experienced, who were foolish and disobedient, to persuade us to be "gentle, showing all meekness;" and he beseeches the Corinthians "by the meekness and gentleness of Christ," as a thing very winning, and of dear and precious account. Let "the same mind" therefore be in us, not only which was, but which, as we find to our comfort, still is in Christ Jesus. That we may not forfeit our interest in His meekness, let us tread in the steps of it; and as ever we hope to be like Him in glory hereafter, let us study to be like Him in grace, in this grace now. It is a certain rule, by which we must all be tried shortly, that "if any man has not the Spirit of Christ," that is, if his spirit is not in some measure like Christ's, "He is none of his." Rom. 8:9. And if we are not owned as His, we are undone forever.

WHEN MEEKNESS IS SPECIALLY REQUIRED

The rule is general—we must show "all meekness;" but it will be useful to observe some special cases to which the Scripture applies this rule.

1. We must give reproofs with meekness. It is the apostle's direction, "If a man is overtaken in a fault," that is, if he is surprised by a temptation and overcome, as the best may be, if God leaves them to themselves, "you which are spiritual, restore such a one in the spirit of meekness." By the spiritual man, to whom he gives this rule, he means not ministers only; doubtless it is a rule to private Christians: all that have opportunity must reprove, and all that reprove must do it with meekness. You that are spiritual, if you would approve yourselves so indeed, actuated by the Holy Spirit, and minding the things of the Spirit, be careful in this matter. Especially let those that are Christians of the highest form, that excel in grace and holiness and the best gifts—such are called spiritual, in distinction from babes in Christ, 1 Cor. 3:1—let them look upon themselves as obliged, in a more peculiar manner, to help others; for where God gives five talents, He expects the improvement of five; the strong must bear the infirmities of the weak. The setting of a dislocated joint or a broken bone is, for the present, painful to the patient; but it must be done, and it is in order to the making of broken bones to rejoice. Now this you must do with the spirit of meekness, with all the candor and gentleness and convincing evidences of love and kindness that can be. The three qualifications of a good surgeon are very requisite in a reprover: namely, to have an eagle's eye, a lion's heart, and a lady's hand; that is, to be endued with a great deal of wisdom and courage and meekness. Though sometimes it is necessary to reprove

with warmth, yet we must never reprove with wrath, "for the wrath of man works not the righteousness of God."

There is an observable difference, but no contradiction between the directions Paul gives to Timothy, and those he gives to Titus in this matter. To Titus he writes to "reprove sharply," and to "rebuke with all authority." To Timothy he writes "not to strive, but to be gentle;" to reprove "with all long-suffering." The reason for this difference may be found in the different temperament of those they had to deal with. Timothy was among the Ephesians, a tractable, complaisant people, who would be easily managed, and with them he must always deal gently. Titus was among the Cretians, who were headstrong, and not to be wrought upon except by sharper methods. Thus, in reproving, a difference must be made; on some we must "have compassion, and others save with fear," but never with anger, "pulling them out of the fire." Or the reason for the different instructions they received may be found—as Gregory, one of the ancients, assigns it—in the different temperament of Timothy and Titus. "Titus was a man of a very soft and mild temperament, and he needed a spur to quicken him to a necessary sharpness in his reproofs; but Timothy was a man of a more warm and sanguine temperament, and he needed a bridle to keep him from an intemperate heat in his reproofs;" and then it teaches us, that those who are naturally keen and fervent should double their guard upon their own spirits when they are reproving, that they may do it with all meekness.

Christ's ministers must be careful, while they display God's wrath, to conceal their own; and be very jealous over themselves, lest sinful anger shelter itself under the cloak of zeal against sin. When reproving—whoever be the reprover—degenerates into railing and reviling and opprobrious language, how can we expect the desired success? It may provoke to contention and to every evil work, but it will never provoke to love and to good works. The work of heaven is not likely to be done by a tongue set on fire of hell. Has Christ need of madmen? or will you talk deceitfully and passionately for Him? A potion given too hot, scalds the patient, and does more harm than good; and so many reproofs, good for the matter of it, have been spoiled by an irregular management. Meekness hides the lancet, gilds the pill, and makes it passable; dips the nail in oil, and then it drives the better. Twice we find Jonathan reproving his father for his rage against David; once he did it with meekness: "Let not the king sin against his servant"—against David—and it is said, "Saul listened to him." But another time his spirit was provoked: "Why shall he be slain?" and the issue of it was ill. Saul was not only impatient of the reproof, but enraged at the reprover, and cast a javelin at him. Reproofs are likely to answer the intention when they manifestly evidence the good will of the reprover, and are made up of soft words and hard arguments; this is to "restore with the spirit of meekness," and there is a good reason added, "considering yourself;" he may fall today, I may tomorrow. Those who think they stand fast, know not how soon they may be shaken and overthrown, and therefore we must treat those that are overtaken in a fault, with the same tenderness and compassion that we would wish to find, if it were our own case.

2. We must receive reproofs with meekness. If we do that which deserves rebuke, and meet those that are so just and kind as to give it us, we must be quiet under it, not quarreling with the reprover, nor objecting to the reproof, nor fretting that we are touched in a sore place; but submitting to it, and laying our souls under the conviction

of it. If reproofs are physical, it becomes us to be patient. "Let the righteous smite me, it shall be a kindness," and an excellent oil, healing to the wounds of sin, and making the face to shine; and let us never reckon that it breaks the head, if it helps to break the heart. Meekness suffers the word of admonition, and takes it patiently and thankfully, not only from the hand of God that sends it, but from the hand of our friend that brings it. We must not be like the reprobate Sodomites, or that pert Hebrew, Exod. 2:14, that flew in the face of their reprovers, though really they were the best friends they had, with, "Who made you a judge?" but like David, who, when Abigail so prudently scotched the wheels of his passion, not only blessed God that sent her, and blessed her advice, but blessed her: not only hearkened to her voice, but accepted her person. Though perhaps the reprover supposes the fault greater than really it was, and though the reproof be not given with all the prudence in the world, yet meekness will teach us to accept it quietly, and to make the best use we can of it. Further, if indeed we are completely innocent of that for which we are reproved, still the meekness of wisdom would teach us to apply the reproof to some other fault of which our own consciences convict us: we would not quarrel with a real intended kindness, though not done with ceremony, and though in some circumstances mistaken or misplaced.

You that are in inferior relations—children, servants, scholars—must, with all meekness and submission, receive the reproofs of your parent, masters, and teachers; their age supposes them to have more understanding than you, and their place gives them an authority over you to which you are to pay a deference, and in which you are to acquiesce, else farewell all order and peace. The angel rebuked Hagar for flying from her mistress, though she dealt harshly with her, and obliged her to return and submit herself under her hands. "If the spirit of a ruler rises up against you," and you are chided for a fault, "do not leave your place," as an inferior; for "calmness lays great errors to rest." "If you have thought evil, lay your hand upon your mouth" to keep that evil thought from breaking out in any undue and unbecoming language. Reproofs are likely to do us good when we meekly submit to them; they are "as an earring of gold, and an ornament of fine gold," when "an obedient ear" is given to a wise reprover. Yes, even superiors are to receive reproofs from their inferiors with meekness, as they would any other token of kindness and good will. Naaman, who turned away from the prophet in a rage, yet heeded the reproof his own servants gave him, and was overruled by the reason of it, which was no more a disparagement to him than it was to receive instruction from his wife's maid to whom to go for a cure of his leprosy. Meekness teaches us, when a just reproof is given, to regard not so much who speaks, as what is spoken.

3. We must instruct gainsayers with meekness, 2 Tim. 2:24, 25. It is prescribed to ministers that they "must not strive, but be gentle to all men," in meekness instructing those that oppose themselves. They serve the Prince of peace; they preach the gospel of peace; they are the ambassadors of peace; and therefore must be sure to keep the peace. The apostles, those prime-ministers of state in Christ's kingdom, were not military men, or men of strife and noise, but fishermen that followed their employment with quietness and silence. It is highly necessary that the guides of the church be strict governors of their own passions. "Learn of me," says Christ; "for I am meek and lowly," and therefore fit to teach you. We must "contend earnestly," but not angrily and passionately—no, not for "the faith once delivered to the saints." When we have ever so great an assurance that it is the cause of truth we are

pleading, yet we must so manage our defense against those who gainsay, as to make it appear that it is not the confusion of the erroneous, but the confutation of the error that we intend. This meekness would teach us not to prejudge a cause, nor to condemn an adversary unheard, but calmly to state matters in difference, as knowing that a truth well opened is half confirmed. It would teach us not to aggravate matters in dispute, nor to father upon an adversary all the absurd consequences which we think may be inferred from his opinion; it would teach us to judge charitably of those that differ from us, and to forbear all personal reflections in arguing with them. God's cause needs not the patronage of our sinful passions, which often give a mighty shock even to the truth for which we plead. Meekness would prevent and cure that bigotry which has been so long the bane of the church, and contribute a great deal towards the advancement of that happy state in which, notwithstanding little differences of apprehension and opinion, the Lord shall be one, and His name one. Public reformations are carried on with most credit and comfort, and are most likely to settle on lasting foundations, when meekness sits at the stern and guides the motions of them. When Christ was purging the temple, though He was therein actuated by a zeal for God's house that even ate Him up, yet He did it with meekness and prudence, which appeared in this instance, that when He drove out the sheep and oxen, which would easily be caught again, He said to those who sold doves, "Take these things away." He did not let loose the doves and send them flying, for that would have been to the loss and prejudice of the owners. Angry, noisy, bitter arguings ill become the assertors of that truth which is great, and will prevail. Our Lord Jesus lived in a very froward and perverse generation, yet it is said, "He shall not strive nor cry, neither shall any man hear His voice in the street." Though He could break them as easily as a bruised reed, and extinguish them as soon as one could quench the wick of a candle newly lighted, yet He will not do it until the day comes when "He shall lead justice to victory." Moses dealt with a very obstinate and stiff-necked people, and yet "my teaching," says he, "will fall on you like rain, my speech will settle like dew." It was not the wind, nor the earthquake, nor the fire, that brought Elijah into temper—for the Lord was not in them—but "the still small voice;" when he heard that, he wrapped his face in his mantle. In dealing with gainsayers, a spirit of meekness will teach us to consider their temper, education, custom, the power of prejudice they labor under, the influence of others upon them, and to make allowances accordingly, and not to call, as passionate contenders are apt to do, every false step an apostasy; every error and mistake, no, every misconstrued, misplaced word, a heresy; and every misdemeanor no less than treason and rebellion: methods of proceeding more likely to irritate and harden, than to convince and reduce gainsayers. I have heard it observed long since, that "the scourge of the tongue has driven many out of the temple, but never drove any into it."

4. We must make profession of the hope that is in us with meekness. "Be ready always to give an answer"—to make your defense or apology, so the word is—whether judicially or extrajudicially, as there is occasion, "to every man that"—soberly, not scoffingly and in derision—"asks you a reason for the hope that is in you," that is, of the hope you profess, which you hope to be saved by, "with meekness and fear." Observe, it is very well consistent with Christian quietness to appear in the defense of truth, and to avow our Christian profession, when at any time we are duly called to it. That is not meekness, but base cowardice, that tamely betrays and delivers up any of Christ's truths or institutions by silence, as if we were ashamed or afraid to

confess our Master. But the office of meekness at such a time is to direct us how and in what manner to bear our testimony, not with pride and passion, but with humility and mildness. Those that would successfully confess the truth, must first learn to deny themselves; and we must give an account of our hope with a holy fear of missing it in such a critical juncture. When we give a reason for our religion, we must not boast of ourselves, or of our own attainments, nor reflect contempt and wrath upon our persecutors, but remember that "the present truth," so it is called, 2 Peter 1:12, the truth which is now to be asserted, is the same with the word of Christ's patience, Rev. 3:10; that is, the word which must be patiently suffered for, according to the example of Him who, with invincible meekness, before Pontius Pilate "witnessed a good confession." A great abasement and diffidence of ourselves may very well consist with a firm assurance of the truth, and a profound veneration for it.

In lesser things, wherein wise and good men are not all in agreement, meekness teaches us not to be too confident that we are in the right, nor to censure and condemn those that differ from us, as if we were the people, and wisdom should die with us; but quietly to walk according to the light that God has given us, and charitably to believe that others do so too, waiting until God shall reveal either this to them, Phil. 3:15, or that to us. Let it in such cases suffice to vindicate ourselves, which every man has a right to do, without a magisterial sentencing of others. Why should we be many masters when we are all offenders, Jas. 3:1, 2, and the bar is our place, not the bench? Meekness will also teach us to manage a singular opinion, when we differ from others, with all possible deference to them and suspicion of ourselves, not resenting it as an affront to be contradicted, but taking it as a kindness to be better informed. Nor must we be angry that our hope is inquired into: even such a trial of it, if we approve ourselves well in it, may be found to praise and honor and glory, to which our meekness will very much contribute, as it puts a luster upon and a convincing power into the testimony we bear. We then "walk worthy of the vocation with which we are called," when we walk "in all lowliness and meekness."

5. We must bear reproaches with meekness. Reproach is a branch of that persecution which all that will live godly in Christ Jesus must expect; and we must submit to it, behaving ourselves quietly and with a due decorum, not only when "princes sit and speak against us," but even when "the abjects gather themselves together against us," and we become "the song of the drunkard." Sometimes we find it easier to keep calm in a solemn and expected engagement than in a sudden skirmish or a hasty rencounter; and therefore, even against those slight attacks, it is necessary that meekness be set upon the guard. If we be slandered, and have all manner of evil said against us falsely, our rule is, not to be disturbed at it, not to render "railing for railing;" but though we may, as we have opportunity, with meekness deny the charge, as Hannah did when Eli over hastily censured her as drunken: "No, my lord, I have drunk neither wine nor strong drink;" yet when that is done, we must, without meditating any revenge, quietly commit our cause to God, who will, sooner or later, clear up our innocence as the light, which is promised in Psa. 37:5, 6; and therefore "do not fret," but wait patiently; "cease from anger, and forsake wrath." Mr. Dod used to charm his friends into silence under reproaches with this: that "if a dog barks at a sheep, the sheep will not bark at the dog again." We only gratify our great adversary and do his work for him when we allow the peace and serenity of our

minds to be broken in upon by the reproaches of the world. For me to disquiet myself and put myself into a passion because another abuses me, is as if I should scratch the skin off my face to wipe off the dirt which my adversary throws on it. When reproaches provoke our passions, which excite us to render bitterness for bitterness, we thereby lose the comfort and forfeit the honor and reward which the divine promise has annexed to the reproach of Christ; and shall we suffer so many things in vain? We also thereby give occasion to those who had spoken evil of us falsely, to speak evil of us truly; and perhaps our religion suffers more by our impatience under the reproach, than by the reproach itself. For what have we the law and pattern and promise of Christ, but to calm our spirits under reproaches for well-doing? Truly those can bear but a little for Christ who cannot bear a hard or an unkind word for Him. If we either faint or fret in such a day of adversity, it is a sign our strength is small indeed. May it not satisfy us, that by our meekness and quietness under reproaches we engage God for us, who has promised that He will "with righteousness judge the poor," the poor in spirit, and will "reprove with equity for the meek of the earth." He that has bid us to "open our mouth for the dumb," will not Himself be silent. And shall we not learn at last, instead of fretting and being exceedingly angry, to rejoice and be exceedingly glad, when "we suffer this for righteousness' sake?" May we not put such reproaches as pearls in our crown, and be assured that they will pass well in the account another day, when there will be an advantageous resurrection of names as well as bodies, in which prospect we have reason to "rejoice that we are counted worthy to suffer shame for His name;" that we are honored to be dishonored for Him who for our sakes endured the cross and despised the shame. It is one of the laws of meekness to despise being despised.

ARGUMENTS FOR MEEKNESS

For the good government of the soul, the judgment must be furnished with proper dictates, or else it will never be able to keep peace in the affections; the emotions of the soul are then likely to be even and regular and constant, when we have established good principles by which we are governed, and under the influence of which we act. We shall select a few truths, out of many which might be mentioned, proper for use as there is occasion.

1. He who is master of his own passions has the sweetest and surest peace. The comfort that a man has in governing himself is much greater than he could have in having people to serve him, and nations to bow down to him. It is certain the worst enemies we have, if ever they break loose and get head, are in our own bosoms. Enemies without threaten only the evil of pain; they can but kill the body, and no great hurt in that as a child of God, if they do not provoke the enemies within, our own irregular passions, which, if they are not kept under, plunge us in the evil of sin. An invasion from abroad does not disturb the peace of a kingdom as much as an insurrection at home; and therefore it concerns us to double our guard where our danger is greatest; and above all keepings, to keep our hearts, that no passion be allowed to stir without a good reason to be given for it, and a good use to be made of it; and then if we be troubled on every side, yet not distressed; perplexed, yet not in despair, 2 Cor. 4:8, 9; offended by our fellow-servants, but not offending our Master; reproached by our neighbors, but not by our own consciences—this is like Zion's peace, peace within the walls. We need to pray as one did, Lord, deliver me from that ill man, my own self, and then I am safe enough. The lusts that "war in our

members" are the enemies that "war against the soul." If this war is brought to a good issue, and those enemies suppressed, whatever other disturbances are given, peace is in the soul, with grace and mercy from God, and from the Lord Jesus. Nehemiah was aware of this, as the design of his enemies, when they hired a pretended prophet to give an alarm, and to advise him meanly to shift for himself; it was, says he, "that I should be afraid, and do so, and sin." Whatever we lose, we shall not lose our peace, if we do but keep our integrity; therefore, instead of being solicitous to subdue our enemies that lay siege to us, let us double our watch against the traitors within the garrison, from whom especially our danger is: since we cannot prevent the shooting of the fiery darts, let us have our shield ready with which to quench them. If we would not hurt ourselves, blessed be God, no enemy in the world can hurt us. Let us but keep the peace within by the governing of our own passions, and then, whatever assaults may be made upon us, we may therein, with the daughter of Zion, despise them and laugh them to scorn, and shake our head at them. Isa. 37:22. Let us believe that in times of agitation and alarm our strength is to sit still, in a holy quietness and composure of mind: "this is the rest with which you may cause the weary to rest; and this is the refreshing;" and it is enough.

2. In many things we all offend. We have this truth as a reason why not many of us should be masters. Jas. 3:2. It would help to subdue and moderate our anger at the offenses of others, if we considered,

1. That it is incident to human nature to offend. While we are in this world, we must not expect to converse with angels, or the spirits of just men made perfect; no, we are obliged to have a communication with creatures that are

foolish and corrupt, peevish and provoking, and who are all subject to like passions: such as these we must live among, or else we would have to go out of the world. And do we not have reason then to count upon something or other uneasy and displeasing in all relations and conditions? The best men have their defects in this imperfect state; those who are savingly enlightened, yet knowing but in part, have their blind side; the harmony, even of the communion of the saints, will sometimes be disturbed with jarring strings; why then should we be surprised into passion and disquiet, when that which gives us the disturbance is no more than what we looked for? Instead of being angry, we should think with ourselves thus: Alas, what could I expect but provocation from corrupt and fallen man? Among such foolish creatures as we are, it must be that offenses will come; and why should not I have my share of them? The God of heaven gives this as a reason for His patience towards a provoking world, that it is in their nature to be provoking: "I will not again curse the ground any more for man's sake; for the imagination of man's heart is evil from his youth," and therefore better is not to be expected from him. And upon this account He had compassion on Israel. Psa. 78:39. "He remembered that they were but flesh;" not only frail creatures, but sinful, and bent to backslide. Do men gather grapes from thorns? "I knew that you would deal very treacherously, and was called a transgressor from the womb." And should not we, much more, be governed by the same consideration? "If you see the violent perverting judgment and justice in a province," remember what a provoking creature sinful man is, and then you will not marvel at the matter. The consideration of the common infirmity and corruption of mankind should be made use of, not to excuse our own faults to ourselves, which merely takes off the edge of our repentance, and is the poor subterfuge of a deceived heart; but to excuse the faults of others, and so take off the edge of our passion and displeasure, and preserve the meekness and quietness of our own spirits.

2. It is incident to ourselves among the rest to offend. The apostle puts himself into the number: We all offend. We offend God; if we say we do not, we deceive ourselves; and yet He bears with us from day to day, and is not extreme to mark what we do amiss. Our debts to Him are talents, our brethren's to us but pence. Think then, if God should were as angry with me for every provocation, as I am with those about me, what would become of me? They are careless in their observance, and perhaps willful in their offense, and am not I so to God? yes, am not I a thousand times worse? Job said, when his servants were provoking, and he was tempted to be harsh with them, "What then shall I do when God rises up? and when He visits, what shall I answer Him?"

And are we not also likely to offend our brethren? Either we have offended, or may offend; we need others to bear with us, and why should we not bear with them? Our rule is, What we would that men should do to us when we offend them, the same we should do to them when they offend us; for this is the law and the prophets. Matt. 7:12. Solomon appeals to our consciences: "For many times also your own heart has known that even you have cursed others." The penitent remembrance of former guilt would greatly help to curb the passionate resentment of present trouble. When the undutiful, rebellious son, in a story that I once read, dragged his father by the hair of the head to the house door, it appeased the anger of the old man to remember, that just so far he had dragged his father; and it seems to have silenced Adonibezek, that he was now treated no differently than he had treated others. Judges 1:7.

3. Men are God's hand; so it is said, Psa. 17:14: "From men which are Your hand, O Lord," or rather tools in Your hand; which are "Your sword." We must abide by this principle, that whatever it is that crosses us, or is displeasing to us at any time, God has an overruling hand in it. David was governed by this principle when he bore Shimei's spiteful reproaches with such invincible patience: "So let him curse, because the Lord has said to him, Curse David." Let him alone, for the Lord has bidden him. This consideration will not only silence our murmurings against God, the author, but all our quarrels with men, the instruments of trouble and vexation. Men's reproaches are God's rebukes; and whoever he is who affronts me, I must see, and say, that by this my Father corrects me. This quieted the spirit of Job, in reference to the injuries of the Chaldeans and Sabeans, though he dwelt as a king in the army; and his power and interest seem to have been sustained when those intruders first made that inroad upon him, and so he could not but see his help in the gate; yet we find him not meditating any revenge, but calming the disturbances of his own soul with the consideration of God's sovereign disposal, overlooking all the instruments of his trouble, thoughts of which would but have mingled anger, the more disquieting passion, with his sorrow; this therefore suffices to still the storm. "The Lord gave, and the Lord has taken away; blessed be the name of the Lord." When his brethren stood aloof from him, his kindred and his friends looked scornfully upon him as an alien; and instead of oil, poured vinegar into his wounds, so that his eye continued in this provocation; yet even in that part of his trouble he owns the hand of God: "He has put my brethren far from me." It is a very quieting truth—the Lord

help us to mix faith with it—that every creature is that to us, and no more, that God makes it to be; and that while many seek the ruler's favor, and more perhaps fear the ruler's displeasure, every man's judgement proceeds from the Lord. Would we but more closely observe, and readily own the hand of God in that which disquiets and provokes us, surely, though we regarded not man, yet, if we had any fear of God before our eyes, that would reconcile us better to it, and suppress all intemperate and undue resentments. In murmuring at the stone, we reflect upon the hand that throws it, and lay ourselves under the woe pronounced against him that strives with his Maker. We know it is interpreted as a taking up arms against the king, if we take up arms against any that are commissioned by him.

4. There is no provocation given us at any time but, if it be skillfully and graciously improved, good may be gotten by it. If we have but that wisdom of the prudent which is to understand his way, and all the advantages and opportunities of it, doubtless we may, quite contrary to the intention of those who trespass against us, gain some spiritual, that is, some real benefit to our souls, by the injuries and offenses that are done to us: for even these are made to work together for good to those who love God. This is a holy and a happy way of opposing our adversaries, and resisting evil. It is an ill weed indeed out of which the spiritual bee cannot extract something profitable, and for its purpose. Whatever lion roars against us, let us but go on in the strength and spirit of the Lord, as Samson did, and we may not only rend it as a kid, so that it shall do us no real harm, but we may besides get food out of the eater, and sweetness out of the strong. As it turns to the unspeakable prejudice of many, that they look upon reproofs as reproaches, and treat them accordingly with anger and displeasure; so it would turn to our unspeakable advantage

if we could but learn to call reproaches reproofs, and make use of them as such for our conviction and humiliation: and thus the reproach of Christ may become true riches to us, greater than the treasures of Egypt.

We are told of an apostate that was cured with the thrust of an enemy's sword; and of one that was happily converted from drunkenness by being called, in reproach, "a tippler." It is very possible that we may be enlightened, or humbled, or reformed; may be brought nearer to God, or weaned from the world; may be furnished with matter for repentance or prayer or praise, by the injuries that are done to us, and may be much furthered in our way to heaven by that which was intended for an affront or provocation. This principle would put another aspect upon injuries and unkindness, and would quite change their character, and teach us to call them by another name: whatever the subordinate instrument intended, God designed it, as our other afflictions, to yield the peaceable fruit of righteousness; so that, instead of being angry at the man that meant us ill, we should rather be thankful to the God that intended us good, and study to answer his intention. This kept Joseph in good temper towards his brethren, though he had occasion enough to quarrel with them: "You thought evil against me, but God meant it for good." This satisfied Paul—in reference to the thorn in the flesh, that is, the calamities and oppositions of the false apostles, which touched him more sensibly than all the efforts of persecuting rage—that it was intended to hide pride from him, lest he should be "exalted above measure with the abundance of revelations;" and there seems to be an instance of the good effect it had upon him immediately upon the mention of it, for within a few lines after, he lets fall that humble word, "I am nothing." We should be apt to think too highly of ourselves, and too kindly of the world, if we did not meet with some injuries and contempt, by which we are taught to cease from man. If we would more carefully study the improvement of an injury, we should not be so apt to desire to revenge it.

5. What is said and done in haste, is likely to be matter for deliberate repentance. We find David often remembering with regret what he said in haste, particularly one angry word he had said in the day of his distress and trouble, which seemed to reflect upon Samuel, and indeed upon all that had given him any encouragement to hope for the kingdom: "I said in my haste, All men are liars;" and this hasty word was a grief to him long after. "He that hurries with his feet sins." When a man is transported by passion into any impropriety, we commonly qualify it with this, that "he is a little hasty," as if there were no harm in that; but we see there is harm in it: he that is in haste may contract much guilt in a little time. What we say or do unadvisedly when we are hot, we must unsay or undo again when we are cool, or do worse. Now who would willfully do that which, sooner or later, he must repent of? A heathen that was tempted to a chargeable sin, could resist the temptation with this consideration, that "he would not buy repentance so dear." Is repentance such a pleasant work that we should so industriously "treasure up unto ourselves wrath against the day of wrath," either the day of God's wrath against us, or our own against ourselves? You little think what a torrent of self-affliction you let in, when you let the reins loose to an immoderate ungoverned passion. You are angry at others and reproach them, and are ready to abhor them and to revenge yourselves upon them, and your corrupt nature takes a strange kind of pleasure in this. But do you know that all this will at last rebound upon yourselves, and return into your own bosom? Either here or in a worse place you must repent of all this;

that is, you must turn all these passions upon yourselves; you must be angry at yourselves, and reproach yourselves, and call yourselves fools, and abhor yourselves, and smite upon your own breasts; yes, and if God gives you grace, take a holy revenge upon yourselves, which is reckoned among the products of godly sorrow, 2 Cor. 7:11; and what can be more uneasy than all this? You take great liberty in scolding those that you have under your power, and uttering perhaps abusive language, because you know they dare not chide you again; but dare not your own hearts smite you, and your consciences chide you? And is it not easier to bear the chidings of any man in the world, which may either be avoided, or answered, or slighted, than to bear the reproaches of our own consciences, which, as we cannot avoid hearing, so we cannot trifle with; for when conscience is awake, it will be heard, and will tell us home wherein "we are verily guilty concerning our brother." Let this thought therefore quiet our spirits when they begin to be tumultuous, that hereby we shall but make work for repentance; whereas, on the contrary, as Abigail suggested to David, the bearing and forgiving of an injury will be no trouble or grief of mind afterwards. Let wisdom and grace therefore do what time will do; that is, cool our heat, and take off the edge of our resentment.

6. That is truly best for us which is most pleasing and acceptable to God, and a meek and quiet spirit is so. No principle has such a commanding influence upon the soul as that which has a regard to God, and wherein we approve ourselves to Him. It was a good hint which the woman of Tekoah gave to David, when she was suing for a merciful sentence: "Please let the king remember the Lord your God;" nor could any thought be more appeasing than that. Remember how gracious and merciful and patient God is; how slow to anger, how ready forgive, and how well

pleased He is to see His people resemble Him: remember the eye of your God upon you, the love of your God towards you, and the glory of your God set before you. Remember how much it is your concern to be accepted by God, and to walk worthy of your relation to Him, unto all well-pleasing; and how much meekness and quietness of spirit contributes to this, as it is consonant to that excellent religion which our Lord Jesus has established, and as it renders the heart a fit habitation for the blessed Spirit: "This is good and acceptable in the sight of God our Savior," to lead a "quiet and peaceable life." It is a good evidence of our reconciliation to God, if we be cordially reconciled to every trying providence, which necessarily includes a meek behavior towards those who are any way instrumental in it. Very excellently does St. Austin remark on Psalm 122: Those please God who are pleased with Him, and with all He does, whether immediately by His own hand, or mediately by the agency of provoking, injurious men. This is standing complete in all the will of God, not only His commanding, but His disposing will, saying without reluctance, The will of the Lord be done. He that acts from an honest principle of respect to God, and sincerely desires to be accepted of Him, cannot but be in some measure adorned with that meek and quiet spirit which he knows to be in the sight of God of great price.

Such as these are softening principles, and as many as walk according to these rules, peace shall be upon them, and mercy; and no doubt it shall be upon the Israel of God.

SOME RULES OF DIRECTION

The laws of our holy religion are so far from clashing and interfering, that one Christian duty very much furthers and promotes another. The fruits of the Spirit are like links in a chain—one draws on another; and it is so in this; many other graces contribute to the ornament of a meek and quiet spirit.

You see how desirable the attainment is; will you therefore, through desire, separate yourselves to the pursuit of it, and "seek and intermeddle with all wisdom" and all little enough, that you may reach to the meekness of wisdom.

1. Withdraw your affections from this world, and every thing in it. The more the world is crucified to us, the more our corrupt passions will be crucified in us. If we would keep calm and quiet, we must by faith live above the stormy region. It is certain those that have anything to do in the world cannot but meet with that every day from those with whom they deal, which will cross and provoke them; and if the affections are set upon these things, and we are filled with a prevailing concern about them as the principal things, those crosses must pierce to the quick and inflame the soul, and that which touches us in these things, touches us in the apple of our eye. If the appetites are indulged inordinately in things that are pleasing to sense, the passions will to the very same degree be roused against those that are displeasing. And therefore, Christians, whatever you have of the world in your hands, be it more or less, as you value the peace as well as the purity of your souls, keep it out of your hearts; and always indulge your affections towards your possessions, enjoyments, and

delights in the world, with a due consideration of the disappointment and provocation which they will probably occasion you.

It is the excellent advice of Epictetus, whatever we take a pleasure in, to consider its nature, and to proportion our complacency accordingly. Those that idolize anything in this world will be greatly discomposed if they are crossed in it. "The money which Michah's mother had," says Bishop Hall, "was her god before it had the shape either of an engraved or a molten image, else the loss of it would not have set her a cursing, as it seems it did." Those that are "greedy of gain" trouble their own hearts as well as their own houses. They are a burden to themselves, and a terror to all about them. "They who will be rich," who are resolved upon it, come what will, cannot but fall into these "foolish and hurtful lusts." And those also who serve their own bellies, who are pleased with nothing unless it is wound up to the height of pleasure, who are like the "tender and delicate woman, that would not set so much as the sole of her foot to the ground for tenderness and delicacy," lie very open to that which is disquieting, and cannot, without a great disturbance to themselves, bear a disappointment; and therefore Plutarch, a great moralist, prescribes it for the preservation of our meekness, "not to be curious in diet or clothes or attendance; for," says he, "they who need but few things are not liable to anger if they be disappointed of many."

Would we but learn in these things to cross ourselves, we should not be so apt to take it unkind if another crosses us. And therefore the method of the lessons in Christ's school is, first to "deny ourselves," and then to "take up our cross." We must also mortify the desire of the applause of men, as altogether inconsistent with our true happiness. If we have learned not to value ourselves by their good word, we shall not much disturb ourselves for their ill word. St. Paul bore reproaches with much meekness, because he did not build upon the opinion of man, reckoning it "a small thing to be judged of man's judgment."

2. Be often repenting of your sinful passion, and renewing your covenants against it. If our rash anger were more bitter to us in the reflection afterwards, we should not be so apt to relapse into it. Repentance in general, if it is sound and deep, and grounded in true contrition and humiliation, disposes the soul to bear injuries with abundance of patience. Those who live a life of repentance, as we each have reason to do, cannot but live a quiet life, for nobody can lightly say worse of the true penitent than he says of himself. Call him a fool—an affront which many think deserves a challenge—the humble soul can bear it patiently with this thought: "Yes, I am a fool," and I have called myself so many a time; "more brutish than any man; I do not have the understanding of a man." But repentance in a special manner disposes us to meekness, when it fastens upon any irregular inordinate passion with which we have been transported. Godly sorrow for our former transgressions in this matter, will work a carefulness in us not again to transgress. If others are causelessly or excessively angry with me, am not I justly repaid for the same or more indecent passions? Charge it home therefore with sorrow and shame upon your consciences, aggravating the sin, and laying a load upon yourselves for it, and you will find that "the burned child," especially while the burn is smarting, "will dread the fire." See Job 42:6.

With our repentance for our former unquietness, we must engage ourselves by a firm resolution, in the strength of the grace of Jesus Christ, to be more mild and gentle for the future. Say you will "take heed to your ways," that you offend not, as you have done, "with your tongue;" and like David, often remember that you said so. Resolution would do much towards the conquering of the most rugged nature, and the quiet bearing of the greatest provocation; it would be like the bit and bridle to the horse and mule, that have no understanding. It may be of good use every morning to renew a charge upon our affections to keep the peace, and having welcomed Christ in faith and meditation, let no unruly passion stir up or awake our love.

3. Keep out of the way of provocation, and stand upon your guard against it. While we are so very apt to offend in this matter, we have need to pray, and to practice accordingly, "Lord, lead us not into temptation." Those are enemies to themselves and to their own peace, as well as to human society, who seek occasion to quarrel, who fish for provocations and dig up mischief; but meek and quiet people will, on the contrary, studiously avoid even that which is justly provoking, and will see it as if they saw it not. Those that would not be angry must wink at that which would stir up anger, or put a favorable construction upon it. The advice of the wise man is very good to the purpose: "Don't take to heart everything people say, lest you hear your servant cursing you;" and it is better for you not to hear it, unless you can hear it patiently, and not be provoked to sin. It is a common story of Cotys, that being presented with a cupboard of curious glasses, he returned his thanks to his friend that had sent them, and gratified the messenger that brought them, and then deliberately broke them all, lest by the casual breaking of them severally, he should be provoked to passion. And Dion relates it, to the honor of Julius Caesar, that Pompey's cabinet of letters coming to his hand, he would not read them because he was his enemy, and he would be likely to find in those who

which would increase the quarrel; "and therefore," as Dr. Reynolds expresses it, "he chose rather to make a fire on his hearth than in his heart."

But seeing "briars and thorns are with us," and we "dwell among scorpions," and "it must needs be that offenses come," let us be so much the more careful, as we are when we go with a candle among powder, and exercise ourselves to have consciences void of offense, nor apt to offend others, nor to resent the offenses of others. When we are at any time engaged in business or company where we foresee provocation, we must double our watch, and be more than ordinarily circumspect. "I will keep my mouth with a bridle," says David, that is, with a particular actual care and diligence, while the wicked is before me, and frequent acts will confirm the good disposition and bring it to a habit. Plutarch advises "to set some time to ourselves for special strictness; so many days or weeks, in which, whatever provocations do occur, we will not allow ourselves to be disturbed by them." And thus he supposes, by degrees, the habit of vicious anger may be conquered and subdued. But after all, the grace of faith has the surest influence upon the establishment and quietness of the spirit: faith establishes the mercy of God, the meekness of Christ, the love of the Spirit, the commands of the word, the promises of the covenant, and the peace and quietness of the upper world; this is the approved shield, with which we may be able to quench all the fiery darts of the wicked one, and all his wicked instruments.

4. Learn to pause. It is a good rule, as in our communion with God, so in our converse with men, "Do not be hasty in word or impulsive in thought to bring up a matter." When at any time we are provoked, delays may be as advantageous as in other cases they are dangerous. "The

discretion of a man defers his anger." "I would beat you," said Socrates to his servant, "if I were not angry;" but "he that is hasty of spirit," that joins in with his anger upon the first rise of it, "exalts folly." The office of reason is to govern the passions; but then we must give time to act, and not suffer the tongue to overrun it. Some have advised, when we are provoked to anger, to take at least so much time to deliberate as while we repeat the alphabet; and others have thought it more proper to repeat the Lord's prayer, and perhaps by the time we are past the fifth petition, "forgive our trespasses, as we forgive those who trespass against us," we may be reduced into temper. It is a good rule, to "think twice before we speak once;" for he that hurries with his feet sins. It was the noted saying of a great statesman in queen Elizabeth's court, "Take time, and we shall have done the sooner." Nor can there be anything lost by deferring our anger; for there is nothing said or done in our wrath but it might be better said and better done in meekness.

5. Pray to God by his Spirit to work in you this excellent grace of meekness and quietness of spirit. It is a part of that loveliness which He puts upon the soul, and He must be sought unto for it. If any man lack this meekness of wisdom, let him ask it of God, who gives liberally, and does not upbraid us with our folly. When we begin at any time to be froward and unquiet, we must lift a prayer to Him who stills the noise of the sea, for that grace which establishes the heart. When David's heart was hot within him, the first word that broke out was a prayer. Psa. 39:3, 4. When we are surprised with a provocation, and begin to be in a ferment upon it, it will not only be a present diversion, but a sovereign cure, to utter a prayer to God for grace and strength to resist and overcome the temptation: "Lord, keep me quiet now." Let your requests in this matter be made

known to God; and "the peace of God shall keep your hearts and minds." You are ready enough to complain of unquiet people about you, but you have more reason to complain of unquiet passions within you; the other are but thorns in the hedge, these are thorns in the flesh, against which, if you beseech the Lord, as Paul did, with faith and fervency and constancy, you shall receive sufficient grace.

6. Be often examining your growth and proficiency in this grace. Inquire what command you have gained over your passions, and what improvements you have made in meekness. Provocations recur every day, such as have been used perhaps to throw you into a passion; these give you an opportunity to make the trial. Do you find that you are less subject to anger, and when angry, that you are less transported by it, than formerly; that your apprehension of injuries is less quick, and that your resentments are less keen than usual? Is the little kingdom of your mind more quiet than it has been, and the discontented party weakened and kept under? It is well if it is so, and a good sign that the soul prospers and is in health. We should examine every night whether we have been quiet all day. We shall sleep the better if we find we have. Let conscience keep up a grand inquest in the soul, under a charge from the Judge of heaven and earth to inquire and due presentment make of all riots, routs, and breaches of the peace within us; and let nothing be left unpresented for favor, affection, or self-love; nor let anything presented be left unprosecuted according to law. Those whose natural temper, or their age, or diseases lead them to be hasty, have an opportunity, by their meekness and gentleness, to discover both the truth and strength of grace in general; for it is the surest mark of uprightness to "keep ourselves from our own iniquity." And yet, if the children of God bring forth these fruits of the Spirit in old age, when commonly men are most froward

and peevish, it shows not only that they are upright, but rather that "the Lord is upright," in whose strength they stand; that "He is their rock, and there is no unrighteousness in Him."

7. Delight in the company of meek and quiet people. Solomon prescribes it as a preservative against foolish passion, to "make no friendship with an angry man, lest you learn his ways." When your neighbor's house is on fire, it is time to look to your own. But man is a sociable creature, and made for conversation; let us therefore, since we must have some company, choose to have fellowship with those who are meek and quiet, that we may learn their way, for it is a good way. The wolf is no companion for the lamb, nor the leopard for the kid, until they have forgotten to "hurt and destroy." Company is assimilating, and we are apt insensibly to grow like those with whom we ordinarily converse, especially with whom we delight to converse; therefore let the quiet in the land be the men of our choice, especially into standing relations and bosom friendship. Observe in others how sweet and amiable meekness is, and what a heaven upon earth those enjoy who have the command of their own passions, and study to transcribe such copies. There are those who take a pleasure in riotous company, and are never well but when they are in the midst of noise and clamor. Surely heaven would not be heaven to such, for that is a calm and quiet region: no noise there but what is sweet and harmonious.

8. Study the cross of our Lord Jesus. If we knew more of Jesus Christ, and Him crucified, we would experience more of the fellowship of His sufferings. Think often how and in what way He suffered: see Him led as a lamb to the slaughter, and arm yourselves with the same mind. Think also why and for what end He suffered, that you may not in

anything contradict the design of your dying Savior, nor receive His grace in vain. Christ died as the great peacemaker, to take down all partition-walls, to quench all threatening flames, and to reconcile His followers, not only to God, but one to another, by the slaying of all enemies. Eph. 2:14, 16. The apostle often prescribes a believing regard to the sufferings of Christ as a powerful allay to all sinful and intemperate heats, as Eph. 5:2; Phil. 2:5, etc. Those who would demonstrate the meek and humble life of Christ in their mortal bodies, must bear about with them continually "the dying of the Lord Jesus." The ordinance of the Lord's supper, in which we show forth the Lord's death and the new testament in His blood, must therefore be improved by us for this blessed end, as a love-feast, at which all our sinful passions must be laid aside; and a marriage-feast, where the ornament of a meek and quiet spirit is a considerable part of the wedding-garment. The forgiving of injuries, and a reconciliation to our brother, is both a necessary branch of our preparation for that ordinance, and a good evidence and instance of our profiting by it.

9. Converse much in your thoughts with the dark and silent grave. You meet with many things now that disturb and disquiet you, and much ado you have to bear them: think how quiet death will make you, and how incapable of resenting or resisting injuries, and what an easy prey this flesh, for which you are so jealous, will shortly be to the worm that shall feed sweetly on it. You will, before long, be out of the reach of provocation, "where the wicked cease from troubling," and where their envy and their hatred is forever perished. And is not a quiet spirit the best preparation for that quiet state? Think how all these things, which now disquiet us, will appear when we come to look death in the face: how small and inconsiderable they seem

to one that is stepping into eternity. Think, "What need is there that I should so resent an affront of injury, that am but a worm today, and may be the food of worms tomorrow?"

A little sprinkling of the dusk of the grave, upon the brink of which we stand, would do much towards quieting our spirits and ending our quarrels. Death will quiet us shortly; let grace quiet us now. When David's heart was hot within him, he prayed, "Lord, make me to know my end."

To conclude, I know no errand that I can come upon of this kind to you, in which methinks I should be more likely to prevail than in this; so much does meekness conduce to the comfort and repose of our own souls, and the making of our lives sweet and pleasant. If you are wise here, you shall be wise for yourself. That which I have been so intent upon in this discourse, is only to persuade you not to be your own tormentors, but to govern your own passions so that they may not be furies to yourselves. The ornament I have been recommending to you is confessedly excellent and lovely; will you put it on and wear it, that by this all men may know you are Christ's disciples? and you may be found among the sheep on the right hand, at the great day, when Christ's angels shall gather out of His kingdom everything that offends. Everyone will give meekness a good word; but in this, as in other instances, honesty is applauded, yet neglected.

Love is commended by all, and yet the love of many waxes cold; but let all that would not be self-condemned, practice what they praise. And as there is nothing in which I should more expect to prevail, so there is nothing in which it will easier appear whether I have prevailed or not: this tree will soon be known by its fruits; so many are the circumstances of almost every day which call for the exercise of this grace, that our profiting therein will quickly appear to ourselves, and to all with whom we converse. Our meekness and quietness is more obvious, and falls more directly under a trial and observation, than our love to God and our faith in Christ, and other graces, the exercise whereof lies more immediately between God and our own souls. Shall we therefore set ourselves to manifest, in all our converse, that we have indeed received good by this plain discourse? that our relations and neighbors, and all that we have dealings with, may observe a change in us for the better, and may take knowledge of us that we have been with Jesus. And let not the impressions of it ever wear off, but, living and dying, let us be found among the quiet in the land: we all wish to see quiet families, and quiet churches, and quiet neighborhoods, and quiet nations; and it will be so if there be quiet hearts, and not otherwise.

Made in United States
Orlando, FL
16 July 2023

35156921R00068